I0843522

BOOMERS AND BROKENNESS

Karen Kellock Ph.D.

Manual for Superior Men

A complete theory based on Einstein physics,
Political Psychology, Systems Theory
and Archetypal Psychiatry.

FORMULA

All success attraction
All disease obstruction
All recovery elimination

You must fast on all three

OBSTRUCTIONS:

People
Habit
Food

BOOMERS & BROKENNESS

When boomers were sickest look what they produced by that BS: prisons and brokenness. Narcissistic Hollywood culture is divorced from reality: violent, decadent and empty seeking to make us just as nasty. You learned lessons from trudging in the mud but they didn't--they even think democrats are good.   Don't minimize betrayal trauma: someone you thought you knew is really a cad into girlie pictures too.

SOCIAL HYPNOTISM

MY SOCIAL CHURCH ERA
HOMESICK FOR HOMELIFE AND FREEDOM
HATING THE HUMAN PARTY
BEING THE WEIRD PARIAH
LOVING CATS AND DOGS INSTEAD
HE CREEPS INTO WOMEN'S HOUSES
SINFUL WOMEN BEG CREEPS TO COME IN
WHY ARE WE INVADED?
DON'T RUIN ELDERING WITH PTSD
THE HELLISH CINDERELLA SYNDROME
CINDERELLA IS ALWAYS TWO AGAINST ONE
YOUR SINS ARE A MAGNET TO MAGGOTS
SINS REFLECT OUTWARD

SOCIAL HYPNOTISM

I can see clearly now, the rain is gone: that's exactly what you'll feel when rid of these bums.

You'll be so **ELATED** when rid of the ill-fated. Not at first but with every new minute you'll get into it.

You may be uneasy at first: "did I do the right thing removing that curse?" Yes, **OF COURSE.**

Being alone is to be on your throne, don't you know? The human critters have held you down.

A "slut" craves attention but after the act has low self-esteem and then wants attention again see.

MY SOCIAL CHURCH ERA

I became a Mormon to please a husband and was swept up into their demands to love humans.

I'm a solitary person who loves being alone with God but they demanded my time with a mob.

They acted like loving God was loving to gab and talk. I lost all solitude and was miserable that's all.

I just wanted to be with my pets not a buncha people and they acted like that was evil.

We are told to love God **FIRST** then our neighbor but they had it in reverse & I was a hater.

It was constant people interaction and I was seen as a problem cuz I just wanted to stay home.

SOCIAL HYPNOTISM

In my Mormon era they'd visit me at home to lecture on how to come along, always on their phones.

As a triple Pisces there's no one more into solitude than me and I was one miserable Mormon see.

In my opinion people addiction keeps you from God man. But to state that was heresy to them.

HOMESICK FOR HOMELIFE AND FREEDOM

I became sickeningly homesick for home, pets, God and angels of thought. I was depressed from mobs.

They'd look at me like I was an evil pariah and would school me on how to come out of it.

I lived in the country, alone in a cabin and that even more attracted them to this strange one.

To me, it was the traditions of men not the word of God. I about went crazy losing privacy to the mob.

This era taught me more about myself than anything I can recall. They were people lovers that's all.

I wanted to stay home to think, meditate and work but that was wrong not putting people first?

Today my husband and I live in our country home all alone and no one bothers us: it's heaven.

HATING THE HUMAN PARTY

No one's judging me to go out to the human party, I can do my thing all day with God's nudging see.

I want God to tell me what to do, not people constantly in their human hullabaloo--it was cruel!

SOCIAL HYPNOTISM

It's the traditions of men versus the Kingdom of God, that's how I see this thing now after all.

They acted like I didn't love God cuz I wasn't a people worshipper, that's the end of this era sir.

There was so much yak-yak there's no way I could think forward or back. I'm so glad I'm free: fact.

Don't get me wrong, Mormons are wonderful neighbors as long as they know you're a die hard loner.

BEING THE WEIRD PARIAH

I didn't like being put in the position of weird pariah, nor being lectured about it neither I'll tell ya.

You don't love God if you don't wanna sit for three hours then listening to the traditions of men?

I'm so much happier now. My mornings, days, afternoons and nights are ALL MINE own, wow!

I'm so happy not planning my day around people events. Its pure joy: God nudging me each minute.

I tried explaining this to them but they wouldn't listen, totally ensconced in the traditions of men.

They cry over the traditions of men. I'm telling you they get positively lugubrious and maudlin.

They think the more they slobber over people the more godly they are, but I wanted to be a star.

Like I said, i learned more about myself in my Mormon era than anything else: a valuable hell.

I want God, not the traditions of men. I want the bible not another book false religions have.

SOCIAL HYPNOTISM

I so missed my pets in this era of mingling with human addicts. I don't like events, it's not my fix.

LOVING CATS AND DOGS INSTEAD

They acted like loving cats and dogs was weird too, an anomaly or even a sickness: it was cruel.

You're supposed to love people not cats and dogs. They went to work on me as if I was flawed.

That was my Mormon era but there were others since. Like living in a small down with social dimwits.

They acted like "being connected" was a measure of your worth. Another hurdle for me, a curse.

People come and go while I stay connected to God. They couldn't see this either, they had no awe.

HE CREEPS INTO WOMEN'S HOUSES

Women talk too much and he just lets her do it: the manipulative creepy man in her house.

As she talks about herself the man finds out her desires, fears, dreams, passions and weaknesses.

By talking too much she learns nothing about him while he learns how to manipulate the woman.

He who flatters his neighbor spreads a net under his feet: he timely uses the right words see.

He manipulates her with the physical [sexual] and he can easily do that since she's emotional.

He brings down her defenses thru calculated conversation: saying what she wants to hear.

SOCIAL HYPNOTISM

By showing up constantly he establishes her addiction through overdosing on approval & affection.

SINFUL WOMEN BEG CREEPS TO COME IN

If she's insecure she does it in reverse: pays him before a job, asks for the rent after not first.

As long as you keep looking back you're frustrated since there's nothing you can do to change it.

Sin [diverse lusts] brings rejection from God but wicked men creeping into the home and it's bad.

"I wish I was dead" was what she said when wanting to be alone but was with people instead.

In my wilderness period I was constantly harassed by invaders. We need a fence or forget it sir.

After being hounded for years now you're famous and alone, in tears? This doesn't make sense sister.

You relocated and got a fence, free of invaders. Now that you're alone you should be happier.

Why am I alone, why does not one ever call me? Because you went out of your way for privacy.

No one insisted more on privacy than you did, so don't be at all surprised at being alone now sis.

WHY ARE WE INVADED?

Why are we invaded in our own houses? Because of our sins and diverse lusts that attract louses.

The bible says it, it works like magic: sinful women attract creeps to their homes & it's tragic.

SOCIAL HYPNOTISM

In my wilderness period they harassed me constantly but now in exile I'm finally alone and happy.

Don't let final solitude make you bitter and lonely, just do your work to achieve the fame finally.

After being in the thick of things with people coming constantly it felt strange to be alone finally.

I had PTSD over what invaders did to me til I realized I had precious solitude and felt really happy.

Over and over their harassments rang in my head til I realized it was over, I was alone instead.

I finally had what I wanted all of my life: to be ALONE dammit so why feel so lonely now, aye?

DON'T RUIN ELDERING WITH PTSD

Life is over in a minute so don't waste it with PTSD thoughts of previous nitwits and dimwits.

f you were to check on em today they'd be just as useless & boring tho' hanging out together ok.

You're alone while they're always together. Who's more useful to society then--you or the socializers?

Having relocated away from the bums, I'm a woman of property & propriety, orderly and happily.

Be happy you escaped and are alone. Enough of this PTSD when they pushed you off your throne.

"Reproductive freedom" means slaughtering innocent babies in the womb. These women are witches, doomed.

THE HELLISH CINDERELLA SYNDROME

SOCIAL HYPNOTISM

The Cinderella Syndrome of horrific abuse by two older sisters is about them conspiring against you.

As they vilify and turn others against the target, it can last for decades and is hardest to get over it.

The Cinderella Syndrome is a devastating form of emotional and financial abuse, a killer too.

This trauma leaves such a profound and lasting impact it shapes the sister target indelibly: fact.

It's an unimaginable violation of boundaries to have family members betray and torment you see.

The older sisters vilify and slander her, robbing the target of her reputation & credibility for sure.

After such an ideal the sister feels profoundly damaged and mistrusting of about all human beings.

Tho' the older sisters passed on the scars remain: many victims channeled it into writing to keep sane.

Please know you are not alone, having endured the betrayals of those closest to you at home.

CINDERELLA IS ALWAYS TWO AGAINST ONE

The Cinderella Syndrome is about two against one: this matrix never changes until they pass on.

Trauma: first from the cruel and manipulative sisters then the alcoholic husband colluding with them.

The level of exploitation, gaslighting and betrayal in this syndrome is heartbreaking--all in the home!

The sisters use her own money which they wrongfully gain control of to bride her husband against love.

SOCIAL HYPNOTISM

She is systematically stripped of all agency, support & autonomy both inside and outside the family.

She is trapped in a toxic web of abuse, deceit and financial control: demoralizing to the core.

As the people closest conspire to undermine, humiliate and keep her powerless it's totally nightmarish.

Isolation, despair and mistrust is fostered within her, feeling profoundly alone and unsafe for sure.

YOUR SINS ARE A MAGNET TO MAGGOTS

Put all persecutors past and present in a bag. Envision God taking em ALL out, tho' they brag.

Stop resenting individuals. They 're no different from any other sinner attracted to your [sin] fall.

When filled with diverse lusts, a sinful woman attracts wicked men creeping into her house.

Put all foes in a bag. The men giving you trouble will go to hell and the women will become old hags.

Your season of treason was directly related to your season of sin, which you've repented from.

It's a relief to see that, so you don't get bogged down with resentment to individual chaps.

I was so pissed off at this guy, that guy...until I saw how my health was going downhill fast, aye.

Read the Psalms to understand that when in sin our HEDGE is down: no protection from clowns.

Both women and men flow in to take advantage of you when in sin: here come the creepers again.

SOCIAL HYPNOTISM

Your sins act like a magnet to maggots. The creeps are instantly attracted in, now never forget it.

It's relieving to know our sins act as a suction cup to users and abusers, to relieve your PTSD sir.

Don't sin then you won't suck em in. You'll also have strength to turn em away for good, again.

SINS REFLECT OUTWARD

SINS are reflected in the external environment. The creeps come around instantly it seems, amen.

If a woman is stuck in her lusts she'll even want the abuser there, that's the paradox sister.

So don't blame him, you begged him to come in. Sin made you lonely and you had no friends.

Abuse, deceit and financial control: that's all she knew but when old she had comfort and gold.

Most women have to go thru this to demand safety & independence: when young she had no fence.

HOBOSEXUALS AND DROP-INS

INVASION OF WOMEN'S HOMES
INVADERS TAKE OVER
PAYING HALF *AFTER* THE MONTH?
THE PRICE OF BEING SILLY
EVERYTHING HAS CHANGED
YOU'RE NOT A SITTING ROOM
GETTING OUTA THE RAIN/HEAT
AVOID DROP INS
FREE AGAIN IS FUN AGAIN
THE INFERIORS RISE UP
AVOID PEOPLE-WORSHIP
PEOPLE ARE DISAPPOINTING
USERS AND TIME-WASTERS
TRUE BENEFIT IS PRIVACY
NEED EM MORE, ENJOY EM LESS
FALSE RELIGIONS ARE PEOPLE-LOVIN'
ONLY GOD TRULY SATISFIES

HOBOSEXUALS AND DROP-INS

INVASION OF WOMEN'S HOMES

Homeless men are now invading women's homes. It's called "hobosexuals" and it's a plague you know.

Women desperate for love and companionship let em in, without boundaries which are life-savin'.

Whether homeless or just dependent, these men butter her up and the desperate female falls for it.

He just wants to get outa the rain or heat but she can't see that, thinking it's a real "relationship".

Once in he takes over and won't leave. When she goes to work he's still there and wants her keys.

Tables have turned: you have handsome fit men [tens] coming into [twos/threes] sloppy/fat women.

She proudly thinks she has a handsome young man when all she is is a hotel [mommy again].

INVADERS TAKE OVER

He abuses her pets or says "we need the TV over there" and she beams with pride about the affair.

Women must see this for what this new thing is: he's using you and taking over your house Miss.

This happened to me way back, beaming with pride and way too immature to wake up to this fact.

It used to be men had their own place see, and of course they'd always set boundaries.

HOBOSEXUALS AND DROP-INS

Women today want love and companionship so go into denial about this kind of relationship.

Women must grow up and set boundaries. He must leave when you say & not bring his buddies.

He wants you to cook and clean and he won't pay half the rent. Gradually he gets as bad as it gets.

A hobosexual works very fast. He wants sex to seal the deal & take control of the house, that's a fact.

PAYING HALF *AFTER* THE MONTH?

If he agrees to pay half the rent [a bad deal] he'll pay if after the month not before, what a heel.

Him being in control of YOUR home feels like fifty-fifty to him but if it was his that'd never happen.

There all handsome and fit while their victims are never it. She can't turn that down/it seems legit.

For the women not have boundaries is so unhealthy, walking around sad and waking up angry.

He asks personal questions right away. Where you work, who you know/how much you make.

He knows just what to say/wasn't born yesterday. She eats it up but a desperate female will pay.

THE PRICE OF BEING SILLY

The price of acting like a silly schoolgirl is heavy but no one can talk her out of hew new steady.

He just wants a place to stay ok, and to get that he'll do and say anything especially a roll in the hay.

HOBOSEXUALS AND DROP-INS

"You're special, like no one I've ever known" he'll say. She laps it up feeling like a queen for today

It's such a sad state of affairs it's a pathetic trend and coming in on us like a hurricane friends.

The trend is based on need not love. The woman has the home [the bait] but he controls the house.

In this atmosphere the status of the cougar [older woman] shoots way up, but watch out!

EVERYTHING HAS CHANGED

Everything has changed and you'd better be ready for it cuz it easily turns dangerous and deranged.

First off, don't let anyone in your house or at least make them leave when you want them to, or lose.

Secondly, see that you're the one with the home so you're the one in control, or be a dam fool.

Learn to set boundaries or you'll lose see. To lose control of your own home happens easily.

For precedents are all: once they've "moved in" it's hard to roll it back, even with your girlfriends.

Use my expression: "home is ALL–where I walk TALL." That is no longer the case with their control.

Don't let people drop by to charge their phone or use the bathroom. You're not a gas station!

YOU'RE NOT A SITTING ROOM

Don't let people use you as a sitting room for them and their friends. Boundaries are essential, amen.

HOBOSEXUALS AND DROP-INS

Call first: don't let em drop by or use you as a pit stop. Notice how they always come at lunch?

You're not a saint for giving up your home. You're a dam fool cuz you're now mentally ill/can't grow.

Home is solitude and protection from others. It's your renewal like a cozy bed of feathers.

GETTING OUTA THE RAIN/HEAT

Girl, they'll say anything to get outa the rain and heat. But you can't see that even if he's a cheat.

Invading peoples homes: that's the horrible thing about wars. It's happening now & you see stars.

The victim will start to make excuses for her visitor, her tenant: busybody, user, lover, obligant.

She'll start to fix him breakfast before she leaves for work for he's tired and is NOT a jerk.

The sicker victims will lend him her car keys and credit cards, for he said he'd pay her back later.

The more she gives the more he takes until he's taken over completely like a ravaging viper snake.

AVOID DROP INS

If there hadn't been a problem you wouldn't have dropped em. Don't look back, just go on.

They saw you as superior so couldn't resist treating you like a joker but now you're on top again sir.

They think they're better than they are, it's called the effect of Dunning-Kruger so drop em sir.

HOBOSEXUALS AND DROP-INS

They saw you as superior so couldn't resist fiddling with your psyche but you know about losers.

FREE AGAIN IS FUN AGAIN

You're free again so relax and grow. They'll never find someone of your caliber, that's all I know.

They devalued on the way to discarding you. But you beat em to the punch by your eschew.

They couldn't resist jerking you around, how they had fun! But now they lost cuz you dropped em.

Discard them before they discard you: That's the gem in your tool kit after the previous hullabaloos.

You got weak under their beak so they had a party calling you a freak but now you can speak.

When they had you over a barrel they demanded more but you squeezed out to a new life galore.

THE INFERIORS RISE UP

The inferiors actually thought you needed em but you proved em wrong while having a ball hon'.

The more victimized you were by previous narcissists who discard the smarter/wiser you are.

You get good at discarding discarders until it takes very little to dump then move on to rewarders.

Give em an inch and they'll use you up til there's nothing left. Get boundaried: take it from me kid.

They always assume they're more important than they are. Give em an inch and they demand more.

HOBOSEXUALS AND DROP-INS

Pay em off & be lucky you're free again. Don't answer their calls/emails & think: I don't know them.

They're so conceited they think you're using THEM. You can predict their discard after devaluation.

AVOID PEOPLE-WORSHIP

Beware of people-worshippers. They don't give a thought to God and call themselves lovers.

All they do is talk of other people, so unself-aware. And you're supposed to listen to them, beware!

You're so advanced and above em you could never explain yourself so why try, just drop em.

You're so advanced they just hate you. They could never understand so go on and eschew.

They call you a hater but they're the biggest haters you know. Forget em, you've no time to blow.

Drop the idiots to make room for others who will benefit. You're wasting time so forget it.

The more alone you become the more room you have to attract higher to your cause and what fun!

While waiting for the higher, clean out your desk and every drawer: soon you'll come to that hour.

It was people who made you a basket case. If left to your own fate you woulda been great.

PEOPLE ARE DISAPPOINTING

People are so disappointing you lost your godly anointing [their devaluing was so depressing].

HOBOSEXUALS AND DROP-INS

You lose nothing by just paying them off for now you have the solitude to do great things.

While waiting: declog the basement, throw/give away your accumulation and become empty man.

The more empty you become the more mass attractions will come and that's the truth, in sum.

USERS AND TIME-WASTERS

People are users and time-wasters so don't let em drop by anymore or continue as a dam loser.

Do they ever bring you anything of good use or just use you up while feeling YOU'RE the benefiter?

A good way to get rid of people is to put em to work when they get there. Make a list, here!

They have nothing better to do so drop in to see you. These are the worst influences, really Sue.

The world is your oyster as long as you stay open sir. But these users waste your time, the losers.

We're here for a minute then we're gone, that's it. Don't waste your time letting users in to ruin it.

They actually think you want em to come. Like you have nothing better to do: it's an insult son.

I've been around the block and what I've written above are my biggest lessons in life, Dr. Kellock.

TRUE BENEFIT IS PRIVACY

The biggest benefit people can give you is PRIVACY: freedom from other influences see.

HOBOSEXUALS AND DROP-INS

Don't get involved cuz when you try to pull away they may get violent. I mean what I say man.

I mean it, get a list ready of jobs they can do when they come. They'll never come again--have fun!

They only drop by to gossip and snoop to feel better about themselves. That's the scoop kids.

NEED EM MORE, ENJOY EM LESS

You need them more while enjoying them less. That's people addiction: it makes you depressed.

I too was guilty of people-worship while not praising God enough and it got me nowhere: just fluff.

I too was leery of disapproval while bending over backwards for them too but I escaped, whew!

You escape then spend years of PTSD thinking what you shoulda said: hey, get out the lead.

I understand it all to well for I too was in hell. By my visitors who devalued me in my empty shell.

Why fear loneliness when that is the ONE thing you need to find God your Father & heavenlyness.

FALSE RELIGIONS ARE PEOPLE-LOVIN'

False religions equate people love with being godly and this has caused mental illness, truly.

Escape and they'll write long letters as to how they're right and you're wrong: that's the throng.

Here they were the ones bothering you and now you get their long letters on how you're nothing too.

HOBOSEXUALS AND DROP-INS

This is their song: let's try to get along, when all you want is to be alone, that is your only throne.

They think "being nice" is the only godly thing when it's being alone with God but do they ever think?

The truly godly loves being alone on his throne and rarely seeks out people thru emails or phone.

ONLY GOD TRULY SATISFIES

His Father God wholly satisfies him so why seek people to "fill the gaps" or pass the time friends?

Follow the lives of great saints. Were they constantly on the phone chatting or gossiping you think?

While it seems lonely at first after dumping them soon you'll be so happy you won't remember em.

The wicked say "faith alone" but Psalms reads: only by repentance does He establish our throne.

THEY ARE IMMATURE

VERY FEW ARE YOUR MENTORS
PEOPLE AND LOVE ADDICTION
THEY ARE "WELL CONNECTED"
RECOGNIZE HUMAN IMMATURITY
THE POWER IS IN INDEPENDENCE
THOSE SOCIAL MOVIES
JUST LOVE DOG AND GOD
THEIR LACK OF SELF-AWARENESS
STOP LOOKING FOR LIKES
LONELY PEOPLE ARE ALL ALIKE
THE IMMATURE DELAY YOU
YOU EXPERIENCE HORRIBLE THINGS
LEARN THE LESSON OF KINGS
TOO MATURE FOR SOCIAL MEDIA
KINGS/QUEENS NEED FOREMEN
LET THIS WHIRLWIND PASS

THEY ARE IMMATURE

You are too mature for those people. It's always a thing where water seeks its own level with the devil.

Think beyond these people dragging you down. They are bores & you have a destiny full blown.

You are beyond mature. You're old & wise person in a young body & these people are bores for sure.

The pointless things they say are wasting your time. You've got world discoveries to make, aye.

You outgrew them, as your maturity got you into a new season with God. Now delete the flawed.

What holds us down? Other people. What creates mental illness? People and the devil.

VERY FEW ARE YOUR MENTORS

Very few can act like your mentor and really help you up sir. Most wanna suck you dry, they are users.

It took me decades of being dragged down to see this major truth: that independence is it Sue.

Your maturity caused God to spiritually elevate you like never before so let him do it, not just endure.

They'll use you up then kick you to the curb. People come and go so stop worshipping man sir.

People worship: They need each other like they need air to breathe. Need em more but enjoy less see.

It's such a joyous release just to need God. No more ups and downs but just see clearly, awed.

THEY ARE IMMATURE

PEOPLE AND LOVE ADDICTION

The minute they meet em they want them back son. It's such a serious drag called love addiction.

They actually think that people-love is being godly, while they leave God out completely.

When you meet em all they talk about is other people. It's a bore to us who love God/hate all evil.

THEY ARE "WELL CONNECTED"

They talk about how "well connected" they are while there's no connection to God for sure.

They don't wanna stay home and enjoy solitude. They love cruises surrounded by crowds Sue.

You're entirely different from them, don't you see that? You need to revel in that not mal-adapt.

Let them go to the clubs and chit-chat. That's not where you're at for it definitely falls flat.

This is your season of rising above this foolishness. You're now seeking one thing: independence.

I can't stand it and really, you can't stand it either. You just haven't recognized this people fever.

RECOGNIZE HUMAN IMMATURITY

You will now recognize the immaturity of people, even your own ones growing up who knew you.

They are held down their entire lives by others while you have been catapulted up by your Savior.

They're like sticky glue and I literally had to relocate to start anew: a fresh breeze like never I knew.

THEY ARE IMMATURE

Of course they can't understand you now, for your level of maturity is way beyond you age: wow.

Today is Sunday, the Sabbath day. It's a day you keep for God but do any of them think that way?

God gave you wisdom, by the power of His holy spirit. It's a bright light shining in you, not dimwits.

THE POWER IS IN INDEPENDENCE

That power is for independence, not being stuck and down with people who only wanna dim it.

That's all I gotta say to you on a Sunday. It's a day of getting close to the only One who matters ok.

God wants more of your attention this season so He can sharpen your mind spiritually, for a reason.

Imagine yourself winning a hundred million suddenly: this is tantamount to this elevation spiritually.

Detach from this sticky glue situation and transcend to the skies of spiritual and mental elevation.

You don't **NEED** these people you think you do. That's just a demonic addiction you're proned to.

This is just the way it is and always was. You just couldn't see it but lost years are the cost.

Watch out tho', for this independence will be even more attractive to them and they'll flood in.

THOSE SOCIAL MOVIES

You'll stop watching movies where there's so much chit-chat and bantering back and forth: bores.

THEY ARE IMMATURE

Give them something that you love and adore and they won't appreciate it at all, that's the score.

If you wake up feeing eerie and lost, think back to who you were with and you'll see the high cost.

Love addiction is the most powerful and hard to get over. Tears on your pillow: what a bummer.

They don't appreciate what you've done, they only want more--thinking they deserve it all forever.

JUST LOVE DOG AND GOD

Give up on people and just love your dog and God. That sounds crazy to people worshippers, flawed.

Get away from people who cause you to stumble into things God already delivered you from hon'.

These people don't want you to be the leader God called you to be and it's very serious see.

You are their leader and mentor, you are mature--and God's gonne prosper you forevermore.

All they want is likes/comments son and if they don't get em it's a reason for all day long depression.

THEIR LACK OF SELF-AWARENESS

Their lack of self-awareness and people dependence is shown by their social media stresses.

God says: "I'm the One who puts one up and another down": success from no one else around.

They can't help where they're at. And they won't change no matter what you say in letters or chat.

THEY ARE IMMATURE

They're gonna relapse right back to cocktails/smokes to cover up what you said about their yokes.

So forget them, you're on your own. Don't be so afraid of fulfilling your own destiny being alone.

You're all alone and thank God you are. Stop trying to get em on to join on the way to being a star.

STOP LOOKING FOR LIKES

Stop looking for likes: give up on facebook and all of em. Think higher to destiny & success friend.

You don't need Facebook for no one really cares anyway. They don't even care to know you ok.

The realization that no one cares is quite an insight to stomach but it clears the way for dumb luck.

These are insights to be gained from all of us for they clear the way for much higher purpose.

You're on your own, get that thru your head. It was that way anyway tho' you wanted them instead.

If you look back, all your problems stemmed from other people. Did ANY of them start with you?

LONELY PEOPLE ARE ALL ALIKE

Lonely people are all the same while all you really need is someone to run errands/pay the bills ok.

You're so dependent on the phone ringing to feel confirmed but ringing bothers the busy/mature.

They're depressed all day cuz no one answered their emails/calls. They even cry over it, wow.

THEY ARE IMMATURE

For the older scholar it's about mental transport not so much traveling, going to clubs or social sport.

We travel in our head and watch movies about the sillies rather than actually doing these things see.

I'd much rather stay in comfort watching travel logs then deal with cab drivers and loud crowds.

Immature people cause stagnation/delays in life, either cuz they refuse to grow or can't see/ aye.

Our God does not like people holding His children back and there's always a karma to this in fact.

THE IMMATURE DELAY YOU

The immature delay you without a thought. Especially if you pay em first, they're giddy and off.

You repented of sins and God said: it's time for new in your life. That's why they don't call, aye.

There's new people who need you now. They need you to pray, educate and fast on their behalf.

So let em go, let em go, let em go. No more being on the begging end like you've been until now.

Free of drags you can be a beacon of light you're meant to be. No more waking up mad/sleepy.

The immature are a terrible drag and sleep-destroyer. You have been on the begging end sir.

You are the light and salt of this world. You will do great things now that God removed boys/girls.

YOU EXPERIENCE HORRIBLE THINGS

THEY ARE IMMATURE

You experienced horrible things knowing those people. You put up with, tolerated & witnessed evil.

Because of this delay/terrible drag you grew for the better. Not one minute was wasted sir.

Though it seemed they just wanted to make things hard for you, much of it was just immaturity Sue.

Tho' you're exhausted from mal-adapting to the inferior now you'll spring right back up, far better.

LEARN THE LESSON OF KINGS

For you've learned the lesson of the king: you need a foreman cuz you can't work with earthlings

They're immature so any attempt to adapt ends in exhaustion: it's always a folie a deux situation.

God wants you in perfect peace so don't focus on these people again or you'll be back in exhaustion.

They automatically have spite or envy cuz you're the boss and they always resent that inevitably.

Thirty years have passed and it shows on their face while you've gotten better and ageless.

You're gonna do great things now, so take the high road and don't engage in drama with the toads.

Releasing immature people always brings great delight, like a giant enema or freedom from strife.

TOO MATURE FOR SOCIAL MEDIA

You're too mature for social media now: that's why you were blocked from facebook so let it go.

THEY ARE IMMATURE

What do you need social media for? Just do your work for God and enjoy the quiet after the war.

Mal-adapting to the drags has made you greater than ever before. God's proud of His son/daughter.

After releasing my immature drag I felt giddy and elated with delight. It's always that way for knights.

The immature don't call when they should and don't reply. Frustration always envelopes you, aye.

KINGS/QUEENS NEED FOREMEN

When you're in power you need a foreman to deal with inferiors. That's our solution forever and ever.

I won't hire again, especially on internet. It always ends in feeling scammed and disappointment.

Once rid of the creeps don't think of em again. Don't drag your precious godly mind down man.

They lead aimless lives based on fulfilling whims of the moment but you have goals like a monument.

Watch movies of the silly herd & you'll understand why your rebelled and true reality you preferred.

Their day is taken up adapting to each other--every move they make--while you're way up here.

YOUR OLD HIGH SCHOOL FRIENDS

Your high school friends show their age while you've become ageless, even more thru the years ok.

The worst possible thing is taking advice from these people. They think reverse from truth [evil].

THEY ARE IMMATURE

With every move adapting to each other they're totally removed from true reality sir.

Remove yourself from that social matrix and be sucked into God's vortex of truth free of lunatics.

The worst thing was when they'd drop by. It was a frustrating interruption in God's/my plans, aye.

LET THIS WHIRLWIND PASS

Let this whirlwind pass like it never was. Let them go on their cruises and socials while you progress.

Not only do they totally adapt to each other, they take each other's views, entirely stupid too.

Let them age and die in their swill while you stay in God's presence: wise, ageless and well.

Let them adapt to each other and stay down/dumb while you adapt to God and will have won.

Think of times you were surrounded by a crowd. Whether family/friend your views weren't allowed.

Oh, the petty criticisms of the dumb! They picked you apart out of pure spite and jealousy hon'.

BOOMERS AND BROKENNESS

LIBERALS ARE EVIL BULLIES
PTSD FOR LIFE FROM THEM
LEISURE IS MOST IMPORTANT
EQUITY OF OUTCOME IS THE PROBLEM
DESTROYING THE FREEDOM TO DOUBT
AGING IS SAGACITY NOT THIS SAD STATE
A TWISTED AND PERVERSE GENERATION
TOXIC SHAME PUT ON YOU
SHAME FROM ABANDONMENT
SHAME LEADS TO CHAOS
SHAME DUMPED BY CHUMPS
SHAME AND FLASHBACKS
WOLVES DIE FROM PACK SEPARATION
STOCKHOLM SYNDROME IS DENIAL
THE CURE IS AWARENESS AND BOLDNESS
LUMINARIES LIGHT THE DARKNESS
THIS IS WHY WE'RE HERE
ADULT BODIES, CHILDREN'S BRAINS
TRAUMA: CONTROLLING THE ENVIRONMENT
RAGE RESTRAINT AT CHAOS
SOLITUDE IS AN ACHIEVEMENT
STAY IN BUBBLE OR TROUBLE
BEING UNPOPULAR BUT RIGHT
I'M ATTRACTED TO YOU BUT...
UNREQUITED LOVE

BOOMERS AND BROKENNESS

SO INTENSE WE WANT ESCAPE
BE PUTTY IN GOD'S HANDS
GOD'S LOVE WAS WHAT I WANTED
DON'T PUT ME IN A BOX
EXPECT WAR EITHER WAY
LATE STAGES OF SOCIETY: BIZARRENESS
BILLIONAIRES ARE LEFT WING HIPPIES
INDOCTRINATING CHILDREN
IDEOLOGICALLY AND MORALLY BANKRUPT
MEN WANT LITTLE LADIES
GUILT IMPLANTS
UNIVERSITY CRIMINAL ENCLAVES
EVIL IN AUTHORITY
FILTHY DEBAUCHED POP CULTURE
OUR GUY THRIVES IN MAYHEM
CHILDISH DEMOCRATS ARE LOSING LUSTER
TWO AMERICAS: CRAZY COASTS & HAPPY FARMERS
CULTURAL PSYCHOLOGY IN STATES
GREAT LEADERS CAN TAKE IT
OLD HIPPIES NEVER GIVE UP
POLITICS TO KEEP INFERIOR OUT
GEORGE SOROS BIG BUX TO SAY TRUMP SUX
SWEPT UP INTO PC CULTURE: DON'T KNOW ANY BETTER
VICTIMIZED IDENTITY CAN'T SUCCEED
IT'S SOLITUDE VS. SOCIAL
MAINSTREAM MEDIA IS THE ENEMY

BOOMERS AND BROKENNESS

LOSERS CAN'T GET OVER IT
TRUMP-HATE PUTS EM OUT OF GRACE
IT'S A SPIRITUAL FIGHT: GOOD VS. EVIL
BOOMERS: CONSEQUENCELESS HEDONISM
LIBERALS PAINT A FALSE REALITY
WHINERS ARE MALADAPTIVE LOSERS
EVEN GRANDMOTHERS TALK ROT
OPINIONS ARE SIMPLY GROUP IDENTITY
HOW TO ADAPT TO CRAZIES: ISOLATION
EASILY BEND A DEMORALIZED POPULATION
NEW MCCARTHYISM
SYCOPHANTS READING OFF SCRIPT
LIBERAL HOGWASH: JOY, LOVE & HAPPINESS
ONLY THE DUMB ARE RABBLE-ROUSED
SPOT THE BIGOT!
SPEECH IS VIOLENT? WE WON'T BE SILENT
LEFT ALIGNS WITH IRAN
FRUIT AND GRAINS
ARNOLD EHRET: ACID IS MUCUS
PUMPERNICKLE IS ACID BINDING!
CORN AND SPUD ARE ACID BINDING
80-10-10 WORKS BEST? FRUIT/STARCH
FRUIT AND CHEESE OR GRAINS
JUST PERUSE YOUR WORK
KEEP WRITING UNTIL THAT MOMENT

BOOMERS AND BROKENNESS

LIBERALS ARE EVIL BULLIES

Feminists are evil bullies by what they ask of flying monkeys when it comes to punishing enemies.

Go thru something like that & never come out of it, not until last breath are you done with it.

The boys who tormented me/changed my brain are now in their fifties and unaware of this see.

A hypersensitive artistic empath suddenly surrounded by loose canon boys wanting a target.

That experience being their target taught me more than a library of books about the youth/kooks.

The problem is trying to be a pal--that's not gonna work cuz you gotta draw lines with guys/gals.

Once freedom is lost and later regained you never stop writing about it seeing its the whole thing.

You get used to everything going wrong & don't expect anything going right-- that's the old life.

Madness unleashed respects neither reason nor boundaries. War is hell but also treachery.

I was psychologically conditioned into passivity. I lost all my audacity, the thing making me me.

Grandiose dreams lie buried in the rubble of destroyed cities. Arrogance ends in ruin all thru history.

BOOMERS AND BROKENNESS

I curbed my impatience and waited for times to turn. They always do eventually then we're first.

PTSD FOR LIFE FROM THEM

I wasn't gonna write anymore, wanted to retire. But it still pours out like it's happening this hour.

To be imposed on like that--like you're just supply. What a lesson for a future leader, aye.

They all wanna piece of me so I draw lines and that makes em despise & start rumors/lies.

You drawing lines is experienced as rejection and that triggers an inner explosion of rage son.

They're so bored, empty and lonely they wanna take over your home see, a hangout for free.

Unwanted/uninvited guests drove me so crazy but now are psych events to write forever about.

It has to do with independence/dependence, identity, creativity, time managed properly, happy.

My answer to them never letting me finish my sentences was to be terse, laconic and wise.

LEISURE IS MOST IMPORTANT

The greatest ingredient to genius is LEISURE cuz that's when you get your greatest treasures.

But leisure is blocked by all the crap we have to deal with, mostly with workers or relatives.

Chalk it all up to periods of mental illness, that's all. We get physically sick, we get mentally ill.

BOOMERS AND BROKENNESS

True genius is characterized by capacity for leisure but would-be genius works compulsively.

Key to Female Success: Find a husband who will allow you privacy and solitude to work in bliss.

Not a "partner". Whoever said "partner?" That's stupid. This is connubial bliss: marriage.

Find a man who will give you as much free time and solitude as you want-- that's number ONE.

Completion: Picture yourself floating up in a big balloon taking you way above past into heaven.

EQUITY OF OUTCOME IS THE PROBLEM

The term "equity" means using raw societal power to punish skin color. Steven Miller

False and dishonorable comparisons like the holocaust and January 6 are dishonest but characteristic.

Nothing worse than a concentration camp except you coming over chump. False comparisons, yuk

Liz Cheney's VP dad not legitimately elected and also a crook, a war criminal, a liar and murderer.

Nurtured by violence and motivated by hate the storm troopers and commies are at our gate.

To play on unspoken fear and unconscious prejudice, truth merges with half truth and lies fast.

Jews were isolated, boycotted, humiliated, condemned then neighbors avoided or turned em in.

DESTROYING THE FREEDOM TO DOUBT

BOOMERS AND BROKENNESS

No one dropped more drone bombs on innocent people than Obama, the loving liberal of America.

Hitler had destroyed all freedom to doubt as indicated by book burnings, firings and what not.

The journey to power carried Hitler from gutter to the top and the purist neither drank nor smoked.

Himmler a one-time chicken farmer became head of the dreaded SS. It's true meritocracy vs. violence.

It that chaos a handful of ruthless men triumphed over the timid or those steeped in self-interest.

You think we spent all this money just for parading? Or do you think we will USE this army? Hitler

Failure to withdraw from an impossible situation means your fate is in your enemy's hands.

Hitler lost the war when he made decisions based on emotion [mainly vengeance] not reason.

At the end no one could talk to Hitler anymore if they did not share his own views. WWII

AGING IS SAGACITY NOT THIS SAD STATE

There's this ageist thing where once you hit 70 you're now obsolete, on your way out, effete.

Normal aging: get better & better until one minute you're dead. No decline into sickness instead.

Since most die in their 70s they project that expectancy onto us, elders exploding with creativity.

If I take on your sad stereotype I'll become another sad failing archetype not rise to the top.

BOOMERS AND BROKENNESS

Age was respected in traditional societies. The elders were given the front seat in the senate see.

I couldn't be this way had I not gone thru that and it all fits synchronistically, its right where I'm at.

A TWIATED AND PERVERSE GENERATION

We live in the midst of a twisted and perverse generation: distorted, really weird, dumb.

A stinking dumbed down generation from systematically eliminating morality and religion.

A whole generation twisted and perverted, think of it: everyone alive at that time being lunatic.

God wants us protected in this weird twisted perverted world while we reach it with our words.

As children of God and lights in the world we're to speak boldly to the evil others, boys and girls.

We're not children of the devil like the rest, acting like their father: instigating, blaming pests.

Remote from the suffering he'd caused he sequestered himself, lost his teeth and quickly aged.

The world is filled with killers and liars because their father the devil is the ARCH murderer/liar.

Look at liberals: the devil is the force in them that justifies lying like it's nothing after all.

We are lights in the world--luminaries like moon, stars and sun--thru rebirth and also adoption.

TOXIC SHAME PUT ON YOU

BOOMERS AND BROKENNESS

Tho' a Christian I suffered with shame. I knew I was forgiven but felt this way just the same.

Yes Jesus removes the ugly stain of sin--but this toxic shame comes from the family system.

Yet a little while and wicked will be NO MORE. You will look for them but can't find em anywhere.

Wicked show off like the flourishing olive tree but then they're suddenly cut down, wait and see.

Repent and He gives you desires of your heart while you see the downfall of enemies for a start.

"I don't wanna live anymore" said the elderly victim of sibling abuse from when she was four.

SHAME FROM ABANDONMENT

Toxic shame is a serious concern for survivors of any type of abusive or destructive relationship.

This type of shame goes beyond thinking "I made a mistake"--it is dumped by a toxic person/family.

The dumping of toxic shame on us is very subtle and sneaky and can involve any flying monkey.

Toxic shame judges YOU not the act which someone perpetrated upon you, they go free too.

Many survivors aren't even aware they have toxic shame but I was embarrassment all the time.

SHAME LEADS TO CHAOS

Toxic shame is another "normal" and common trauma response but it can lead you to chaos.

BOOMERS AND BROKENNESS

After marrying a narcissist unawares it was only in social settings his symptoms arose.

While alone we were fine but when others didn't like me he joined their club: a pattern of chumps.

After being so manipulative tho' secret then turning it all around so everything's your fault.

When shame becomes toxic it can eat at you and destroy your life and livelihood quick.

You are not to blame for toxic shame. It has nothing to do with you but patterns handed down ok.

SHAME DUMPED BY CHUMPS

Toxic shame is about OTHER people--malicious dumpers of shame on the good called "evil".

Physical symptoms, emotional distress, nervous system triggers causing fight/flight/freeze/fawn.

Shame makes one feel exposed or want to conceal identity and there are trauma symptoms see.

"You deserved it. It's all your fault, you brought it on yourself"--there's the gaslighting from hell.

They hide behind their masks/crazy making smokescreens and sidekick flying monkeys.

There's no excuse for abuse and there's no excuse for toxic shame either, a worst subterfuge.

Toxic shame causes brain fog, memory loss, anxiety and feeling overwhelmed with life itself.

SHAME AND FLASHBACKS

BOOMERS AND BROKENNESS

Toxic shame triggers flashbacks and memory distortions making you feel even more shame-ridden.

Toxic shame equals chronic pain. Aching joints, backaches, need naps, seeking drug escapes.

Feeling alienated and ostracized--they're all pointing the finger at you, the shame filled and despised.

Signs of toxic shame: Isolation and the inability to participate in society as they should ok.

They isolate because they don't feel safe. Gatherings and functions are chores which they hate.

The toxic shamed won't feel comfortable being themselves having been ridiculed for it.

The shame of this nature causes one to not feel accepted by friends, family or society.

The shame & guilt was laid on you—it is a trauma response. It is not real = not your fault.

WOLVES DIE FROM PACK SEPARATION

Toxic shame is rooted in being abandoned like wolves who die of starvation after separation.

The narcissist wants all attention on him so when YOU get it they inflict toxic shame to deflect it.

Shame is internalized [into all cells] when one is abandoned/ceases to exist psychologically.

Being compassionate with self is cure for the nasty shame-blame game imposed on you from them.

Toxic shame may be so intensified you are paralyzed. Like a lamb to the slaughter, silenced.

BOOMERS AND BROKENNESS

I couldn't be a truth teller when toxic shame silenced me forever due to envy, abandonment or whatever.

STOCKHOLM SYNDROME IS DENIAL

Silencing means living in denial about your past abuse. Even telling the world you love those two.

Shame silenced you so badly you're literally stuck in a denial stage which becomes insanity ok.

The abuse trauma may have hurt so deeply and badly you're stuck in denial, a sort of blackout.

Denial--being literally struck dumb--is a trauma response and I couldn't stand up for myself.

Disturbing memories plague us. It's PTSD to re-experience these horrible attacks in the past.

Shame-based beliefs: you're inadequate, unworthy, defective, a fraud, unlovable, unimportant.

Shame is internalized after dumped on us from others. It's important to keep this central forever.

The toxic mother takes her shame and dumps it onto the child who feels it as guilt for life.

Eating disorders, anxiety, irrational guilt--because it wasn't my guilt to carry, an insight still.

Toxic shame brings perfectionism and attraction to unhealthy relationships, more years lost.

THE CURE IS AWARENESS AND BOLDNESS

The cure is awareness, a trauma recovery coach or just digging deep/seeing how the system works.

BOOMERS AND BROKENNESS

Stop questioning the will and work of God. His work is FOR us, in us and should be from us.

The above verses should relief you sis since you now see it wasn't YOU it was the narcissists.

The world and most whom you've known are EVIL and that's why you've had so much trouble.

Do not fret/be envious of evil doers. Trust in the Lord for they'll fade like the green herb.

Evil doers WILL be cut off but as you wait for the Lord YOU will inherit the land as your fathers.

God gave me three acres and 3 houses on prime view property all cuz I left the evil family.

You look carefully for foe's place but he can't be found, only the humble will inherit the land.

Don't complain, everything is exactly on schedule and you're right where you should be I tell you.

LUMINARIES LIGHT THE DARKNESS

Luminaries light darkness in creation. If it weren't for the salt of the earth it'd be a black cavern.

"...among whom you APPEAR as lights in the world"--we can't be hidden under a bushel, angels.

This is where we need be as children of God, only light in darkness, the one thing holding em up.

Let your light shine before men so they can see your good works and glorify God in heaven.

We're right where supposed to be: in a twisted generation speaking truth and protected see.

BOOMERS AND BROKENNESS

Jesus humbled himself in crisis taking on the attitude of a slave and God exalted him that day.

Work out your salvation with fear and trembling as the holy work is brought to sweet completion.

Pursue holiness to bring your salvation to completion: humble and perfect with good works done.

Is this possible? Yes because it is God working in you to perfection for His good pleasure son.

I never thought little ol' me could pursue holiness until I realize it was God who was doing all this.

THIS IS WHY WE'RE HERE

That's why we're here: to show an evil twisted world the good news of Christ/freedom from turmoil.

We are to rejoice in sacrifices required, like repentance and turning from mockers and liars.

Humbly, holy, lowly and proclaiming the gospel, joyful. But the highest is stop complaining too.

You are not to complain cuz this is where God has you--that should bring relief from the blues too.

Looking back things happened in sequence and it couldn't be any other way so accept this.

We support total catastrophe because catastrophe would bring an end to the system. Gregor Strasser

Idiocracy: literally everything has to be part of the social justice movement.

ADULT BODIES, CHILDREN'S BRAINS

They have adult bodies but children's brains. So when they want something and you block that: IT'S ON.

BOOMERS AND BROKENNESS

He had me so intimidated as he'd rise up in violence. Not hit me but the threat was there and so I truckled.

And here he was just someone I let into my home. He wasn't family or even a friend but a liberal syndrome.

God wanted to teach me about the youth nowadays--at what He put me through I was shocked and amazed.

Flee, they follow. Follow, they flee. This refers to the game of hot and cold: a freeze out with you feeling guilty.

The short cycle is hot and intense but the long cycle is cold and long creating attempted/frenetic resolution.

You can't work with a hot and cold player. They don't have a skill set for a relationship/just wanna feel safer.

How to move forward: find a win. If we can find that win then we can move easily thru a difficult transformation.

It's a severe demotion but everyone has to go through this humbling son--on the day of humiliation.

Being broke teaches you gratitude, appreciation and simplicity. I've been there and it helped immensely.

Older means more time getting the devil out of me or more time becoming just like my greatest adversary.

Something flipped his/her switch and they fell into their bag--ridiculous/atrocious sins from a previous age.

Complex PTSD can be so crippling it's like the guy's in the room. We feel fear, aggravation, doom.

TRAUMA: CONTROLLING THE ENVIRONMENT

The environment is so chaotic the trauma teaches the child how to control it--make it safe and predictable.

BOOMERS AND BROKENNESS

The traumatized child must make sure he has **TOTAL** control of his world to make it safe and predictable.

Over-control is a safety mechanism to be certain chaos is kept away. It's a matter of survival every day.

When the environment again becomes chaotic, rage appears to bring it back-- "the angriest person I ever met".

RAGE signals: I do not want to re-experience the trauma of cheating, anger, damage, imposition, bedlam!

RAGE RESTRAINT AT CHAOS

My reaction to chaos is controlled rage to carefully and quickly bring order back by ejecting the bad.

I reacted with rage at people lying all over my floor--the new chaos so different than I ever knew before.

The only way to stave off harmful chaos is to control everyone around me even those talking behind my back.

But living in liberal Borrego on the main road I had no control. It all imploded on me--hello "street school".

At that early point I didn't even realize I needed privacy let alone how to get/maintain it. I was just a grunt.

When kids dropped by without announcement it triggered those early fears of environmental chaos.

I became so sad in this mess, like a big dark cloud. All I had to do was slam the door but I wasn't that strong.

I already had the rep of being odd, a stranger always alone. So I gave into misery and totally lost my throne.

You just gotta say: "I don't want anyone around, I just wanna be alone"--non-discriminating, ok?

BOOMERS AND BROKENNESS

Cuz if they think you just don't want **THEM** there they'll get violent or calumnious, it must be everyone, hear?

It can be horrible to witness the Day of Humiliation for it's a sudden deflation from arrogance to low station.

SOLITUDE IS AN ACHIEVEMENT

Solitude is an **ACHIEVEMENT** cuz it takes work, strength and dedication to keep em out and truly mean it.

Being alone is a hideous stigma on a woman until she breaks through to higher dimensions, renowned.

Way of the sinner: watch the whoremonger criticize petty things that don't matter so he can feel better.

Going **COLD** is like a rudder to control things so they don't get too intense and then you're hurt badly again.

EMOTIONAL chaos? No way. We're no more raging/gaming children but two intelligent mature adults.

After trauma even seeing one's spouse more than twice a day can be chaotic--for safety it's all subjective/I like it.

I was just a renter in town but was thrown into a social maelstrom automatically without knowing it.

Without firm boundaries, suddenly it was all their network, and all their network--an unvetted buncha jerks.

In any social gathering I feel imposed on immediately. Scrutinized by evil projections unabashedly.

I'm just not interested in that crap and if you are, go ahead. To me it's exhausting, abusive, intrusive, dead.

Lower minds have weird projections to novelty--the etiology of the "evil stepmother" syndrome you see?

BOOMERS AND BROKENNESS

They're just a bear in a corner poked with a stick desperately trying to survive--by being a dam controller, aye?

STAY IN BUBBLE OR TROUBLE

If I didn't learn how to stay in my bubble I woulda been thrown to the wolves, suffocated and smothered.

The most important thing for a genius to learn is his own limitations beyond which he's just a worm.

I don't wanna go to boring parties where they talk about nothing I just want my own thing: free.

When suddenly their devices don't work with you--a rare jewel--they become a poked bear, very cruel.

The destructive narcissist can't have empathy for you, he's too fearful for his own life, a reaction from two.

Blowing hot and cold is the only rudder for control cuz when it gets that intense it's a catastrophe from way back.

It's called STRIFE. He's in turmoil, fear and paranoia--how can he possibly be concerned for your life?

It is dehumanizing to be with someone who controls his reality this way--including everything you say.

A reality-controller is not connecting with how you feel--and so you feel dehumanized and it gets surreal.

After living in non-reality of drunkenness she came into reality while dying and the daughter couldn't re-align.

You don't have to live in the tyranny of past people's projections. You can relocate/never see em again.

When I relocated I never saw any of em again. I doubt they thought of me either--just a phase, era of shame.

BOOMERS AND BROKENNESS

BEING UNPOPULAR BUT RIGHT

I had to defend my right to feel right tho' unpopular. Popularity indicates stupidity not the truly rare.

They can't connect with you/worry about you when they're trying to save themselves vs. mature relationships.

They're trying to save themselves from re-experiencing the trauma, from losing control, from being eaten up.

Understanding these things about people will bring out a new level of empathy in yourself, and it's a relief.

Need understanding that it's not personal--about you--but trauma-based, chaos-based, not rational.

It relieves much stress to realize that even though it feels intensely personal, it's not about you at all.

Do you really want to be in that very unpleasant place where that person's trauma is coming onto you?

Just remember it was the children who beat up Beethoven and who were the basis of the Maoist revolution.

People suddenly rewrite history and facts to support their own emotional agenda, that's the new America.

People who use emotional reasoning thru delusional thoughts will always end gaslighting you--leave em out.

I'M ATTRACTED TO YOU BUT...

The lady said "Yes I'm attracted to you but can't bear the emotional trauma so good luck, I'll bid adieu".

I'm attracted to you but it's just like pie/cake: I may want em but there's a higher principle that says "no way".

BOOMERS AND BROKENNESS

Of course I want you but I don't do what I want. Those are the kinds of women you hate, you even said it.

I don't just give in to my whims, desires, urges like you do. You suffer afterwards while I stay calm/cool.

No we're not gonna "work it through" then become friends. That is purely and utterly ridiculous you fiend!

I don't care what you feel or want--that's not any of my business. Stop telling me that, just deal with it.

The lady said YES I'm attracted to you but i'm gonna let that go now, it doesn't matter what I want said God.

I'm better for knowing you, so I'm leaving with a WIN. That'll ease the transformation and maybe depression.

Man I wish it woulda worked but it just didn't. "It still could" my lower self says cuz I'm human and tragic.

Another time or place, or maybe it's still in the cards. Who knows? I'm staying dreamy but above board.

UNREQUITED LOVE

The perfect answer to relationship problems is to dial him back/yourself UP. That always works, start now.

You're just another tantalizing treat I have to give up before it ever happened. I have to be a grownup, n'espa?

It's deep, profound, frustrating, intense, exhilarating. That's my enduring love for you, my **DESTINY**.

If I'm replaced it'll kill me but that's what happens when detained by circumstances making you unfree.

I don't expect you to wait around, you've got your own life you wanna plan but I'd wait for you forever man.

BOOMERS AND BROKENNESS

SO INTENSE WE WANT ESCAPE

It's too intense, I must escape. But where to? I'm a prisoner of love but what exciting relief from all that hate.

Ok now you know the truth, though I'm sure you knew it before. It's part of the human condition as we pair.

Circumstances, yes: circumstances. They obstruct new plans, with age we don't take those chances.

There are no other options when it comes to you. You are the best and to even know you I feel blessed.

I've told you the truth, no holds barred. I've laid the cards on the table tho' it's still unresolved. I'm sorry love.

That's all she wrote, you know it and I won't write more. It's an all-consuming emotion: this heart I adore.

BE PUTTY IN GOD'S HANDS

I am putty in your hands and that makes me wanna run the other way man but I can't as a prisoner of love.

If it ends before it starts at least I know the extension of my heart and that's worth knowing before I depart.

We don't always get what we want in life--circumstances block or strife--but at least we see eye to eye.

What a strange virtual world where I can lay open my heart to you sir but I don't dare say anything more, ciao.

Of course I fear interviews, decades of work could be undervalued cuza one stupid word/false move.

A time is coming soon when you must relocate. It'll be too dangerous, weird, depressing--bad fate.

BOOMERS AND BROKENNESS

God went before to create a home for me and He'll do the same for you--maybe it's a joint journey.

God works suddenly. When it was time to leave the desert He yanked me out from a shack to a mansion, truly.

I'm handling success like a crate of eggs: not one false move. 112 books are 52,000 perfect tweets/new views.

GOD'S LOVE WAS WHAT I WANTED

God said "I love you/always will love you and you're all I think about" and I felt satisfied I finally got what I wanted.

Like Jesus said to His disciples: "My time has not yet come" yet they continued to push as if they were it.

After knowing you I know what it musta been like in Nazi Germany, terrifying/awful on all levels honey.

Jesus said to His disciples: "My time has not yet come" yet they continued to push as if they had the wisdom.

It's called the Dunning-Kruger Effect: dumb people thinking they're doing it right. Look up: Low IQ and spite.

I woulda stayed right had the devil in you not gotten in me. I always wanted to be alone but you imposed, see?

I need a diet where I'm not hungry/always thinking about food. The fruit diet didn't do this without avo.

I don't like fruit smoothies without nutbutter and coconut cream in them. I just like satiating fat, it's grounding.

So few people I could talk to and you were one. But now we're in a quandary-- let us pray/stay calm.

Please don't misjudge what I do and I'll watch the same. I'm cautious/not a jerk, it's just circumstances ok?

BOOMERS AND BROKENNESS

I'm never bored nor lonely dear, and I'll always have my work. My home too, the lovely views and thoughts of you.

You have no idea the sleepless nights over you: lost love. I hear everyone's been thru this but it sux alot.

I'm not one of those pitiful brazen women fornicating all over town. I don't drive nor ever even leave home!

DON'T PUT ME IN A BOX

Please don't put me in a box with all other women cuz I hate em too! Feminism is perversion, ladies are few.

You're one of the few I can talk to, tho' I've never talked to you. That's the way it is: subliminal/silent too.

These are my love letters to you, so in case I die you'll have em permanently for posterity if need be.

I have my thoughts of you, things you've said, a few pictures and that'll have to suffice, life's not always nice.

I don't watch silly reality shows--I hate em too! I hate it when girls scream and jump up and down: subhumans.

I never leave home unescorted and even then I never wanna go. Only essentials for I'd rather stay home.

I hate going anywhere and I hate parties and all social get-togethers especially Fake Church functions.

Love is the most all-consuming of all addictions, like a trance state. It's pure joy or devastating lows I hate.

If I talk to you I take the chance of you ghosting me so all I can do is not talk to you and that's true dignity.

You seem to want me to be in constant tension and anxiety. You go silent, I truckle--it's how you control me.

BOOMERS AND BROKENNESS

You're just gonna have to read it here cuz then if you ghost me I won't know it and it's no big thing dear.

When things happen it's sudden and in between there's nothin'--that's how it works so keep on truckin'

Never bemoan past mistakes or your age. Things couldn't have happened any other way, it's synchronicity.

Does he have decorum--good taste and propriety--or is he vulgar, gross, obtrusive and just a dam bum?

EXPECT WAR EITHER WAY

If Trump wins, expect war. If Trump loses, expect devastation, communism, replacement, war.

I'm expecting war and devastation. I don't see any other options cuz kids are our future/it's a mess son.

As things get weirder/more dangerous you're gonna have to move. Get outa the city to the country I behoove.

You will love the country: crows in the morning, balmy breeze in the aft, crickets at night, feeling God's love.

Rules of Wokeness: Everyone in group A is exempt from any liability, all in Group B is liable/responsible, see?

The American Dream of buying a single home to raise a family is now seen as greed, selfishness and bigotry.

BLM is a costume white liberals wear to tear down the west which they see as inherently/incorrigibly evil.

Children of the Lie are liberal media, the dem party, the RINO reps, never Trumpers and the black race hustlers.

CRY-BULLYING does nothing but create a temporary gang hell-bent on destroying by which they self-implode.

BOOMERS AND BROKENNESS

There's a false assumption that Obama did more for blacks because of his skin color. WRONG, it was nil.

A WOKE culture is a radically unforgiving one. There is no empathy as we see them all turning on Ellen.

LATE STAGES OF SOCIETY: BIZARRENESS

In the decadent late stages of society, bizarre behavior proliferates and is legitimized, fetishizing pathology.

Pop culture is a threat to the west since it provides our enemies with a justifiable reason to destroy us.

Safe spaces, PC, virtue signaling, gender studies: When did "being cool" become parroting stupidities?

By making our cultural underpinnings completely meaningless (Miley Cyrus) it is easily overthrown and dissed.

The cycles of seasons, moons, empires, nations and peoples: They rise and they fall but now we're shirking evil.

BILLIONAIRES ARE LEFT WING HIPPIES

The vast majority of billionaires are left-wing hippies who want to keep the middle class poor/downstairs.

Education is a weapon whose effects depend on who holds it in his hands and at whom it is aimed. Charlotte Iserbyt

Obama's encouraging protestors to continue the violence. Scary stuff, the ideologues are tireless.

Liberals can't see danger cuz their conscience is seared from their true nature so they love the stranger.

Liberals don't want us to investigate voter fraud, of course not.

It's a culture war. To see what that is see Hollywood scum at their events then listen to media for more.

BOOMERS AND BROKENNESS

If we can't convince them how they're conned, there is no hope. Tell em though you're banned/called a dope.

They can't renege/accept Trump cuz that's admitting what fools they've been and this they can't stomach.

What about the poor folk who are already here? Liberals call them "bitter clingers" cuz aliens they fear.

INDOCTRINATING CHILDREN

Indoctrinating very small children--despicable crime. You won't believe what they're telling them, the slime.

They're telling tiny young kids to kill the racist Trump. This after expelling them for making finger guns.

Liberalism will now become more and more irrelevant and the divisions will get larger as they vent.

When ugliness is venerated as beauty we know we're in the depraved late stages of civilization.

Share: Popular culture does **NOT** represent western civilization--only the great works like Beethoven.

Popular culture is so invasively vulgar it's seen as the reason for terror attacks making us suffer.

Leave empty cultural Marxism for Renaissance: beauty, talent and exalting human accomplishment.

It's been going on at Berkeley, just more inflamed. These things always accelerate, nothing stays the same.

Students are encouraged by faculty and rich dems like Pelosi to "shut it down" and "protest in streets", crazy.

The Free Speech Movement started in 1965 with the hippies but not for the right wing speakers like you/me.

BOOMERS AND BROKENNESS

IDEOLOGICALLY AND MORALLY BANKRUPT

They're not only ideologically but also morally bankrupt while saying we should be more civil and tolerant!

Environmental groups: left wing advocacy orgs with every trendy issue in the same basket (gays, trans, you got it).

Left has no objection to chaos: they accept Jihad and the disasters coming from it but Trump will fight it.

Feminism is the default setting for college age women but it makes them mean, nasty, vindictive vermin.

What man would want them? You gotta subscribe to the natural order eventually: birds and bees in sum.

MEN WANT LITTLE LADIES

What men want is the sweet little lady. Where are they? Crazy, freaky, some brainy but most are shady.

The democrats are telling illegals how to resist the border patrol: They just want anarchy, votes and civil war.

Universities won't fight back but nature abhors a vacuum and it'll come against and destroy them: fact.

Trump threatens to cut federal funding to UC Berkeley after a night of violence. Good for you, do please.

Trump said if no free speech and unstopped violence on innocent people then no federal funds. Fun!

They don't know how gov works nor do they care. They are only self-aggrandizing so Trump, beware!

There's nothing new with anarchy and obstructionism is middle name of democrats, AKA "by any means necessary".

They feel superior without doubt.

BOOMERS AND BROKENNESS

A landslide though only one-third of conservatives voted: The tip of the spear so keep that well-noted.

Corrupt media's against Trump cuz they're owned by multi-national corps who want us poor so they can rob.

Big business hated Donald Trump and loved Hillary but that's changing.

GUILT IMPLANTS

"My job is to make sure they get that they have privilege"

Suppression only makes us stronger.

We didn't elect you to "reach across the aisle" but to do an agenda which comes against the vile.

Trump didn't "fail" he's just not appointing your guys. You lost, you failed so accept it/repent for your lies.

Is there anyone more irrelevant than Glenn Beck right now, saying God told him to vote for Cruz? Wow

Liberals down on USA know nothing about what other countries are like. They are so lucky, but they fight.

The herd mentality without a mind, united as one kind: hating Trump and blind.

Trump doesn't care: He knows he's doing the right thing so let em lie and make stuff up but he'll stay in prayer.

A black person is 2000 x more likely to be killed by another black, than a white/cop/KKK--that's a fact.

If you're a Donald Trump supporter you must stay very close to the police: You are a marked Man of Peace.

It's the same spirit in all us patriots: it's God wanting us to have justice.

Judges aren't supposed to "help people" but interpret the law of good vs. evil.

BOOMERS AND BROKENNESS

Our guy is so strong and smart! He suffered/broke through the log jam of bought off media and hard hearts.

UNIVERSITY CRIMINAL ENCLAVES

The no-action let-em-burn-it-down university is a criminal enclave. It's about to change/they will behave.

Universities now devil worshippers and death lovers: not the whole generation but can goodness be recovered?

You're not paranoid thinking they're out to get you (please!) or those trying to change the world are evil enemies.

Youth: Unable to diffuse anger into music or subculture they turn to the mental ghetto of identity politics.

The pressure to conform to canons of popular taste--or lack of taste--has never been stronger. PJ Watson

Lincoln had federal judges arrested and the best presidents put them down.

Fake polls: left-leaning means lying.

Once we absorb degeneracy our moral filters are irreparably damaged. PJ Watson

Cultural hypersexualization normalizes cheating and betrayal--when everyone else is doing it, it's less shameful.

We love Trump cuz we're sick of being bullied by the word police and love how he said what he pleased.

It's not "see you later, we won" but now we gotta protect our man so he can protect us--we've only begun.

Prepare for the rough months ahead too because Trump's gonna continue to do what he said he'd do.

The Clinton Foundation is the largest unprosecuted charity fraud in the history of mankind. Charles Ortel

BOOMERS AND BROKENNESS

EVIL IN AUTHORITY

The pope likens "conspiracies" to the sexual desire for feces. Not a catholic but a Jesuit communist, jeez.

Left calls Trump "ineffectual" though he's gotten more done in 2 weeks then 8 year under pseudo-intellectuals.

It wasn't that you were an ass in your past but you lacked self so reflected pop culture (no class).

Quit arguing with liberals for what does it help? Save your energy and withdraw into your happy sane self.

Why we love him: Though the press hates him he's completely unencumbered by popular opinion.

Liberals heads are spinning right now. Gaga didn't trash Trump but just stuck to her job and entertained.

Liberals bash GaGa cuz she didn't bash Trump.

Backlash for daring to *not attack* Trump!

FILTHY DEBAUCHED POP CULTURE

Filthy pop culture is last stage of civilization decline, but repentance brings us back like Nineveh (refined).

Trumpism: It's a badge of honor if the leftist press hates him.

Media has a marginalization agenda. Trump

Liberals think all cultures are alike/equal but there's nothing more false: some are good and some are evil.

It's "social hypnotism": how cultures think alike. It's like a herd or flock of birds in perfect unison/flight.

Split between left and right is growing daily. A wide chasm and there's no going back, like a Muslim and an Israeli.

BOOMERS AND BROKENNESS

I'm never arguing with them again. It made me sick and fatigued back then so I'll just talk to smart friends.

Stress comes from arguing with idiots so get healthy by avoiding the hideous, oblivious, lascivious and pitiless.

All negative polls are fake news. DJ Trump

OUR GUY THRIVES IN MAYHEM

Our guy thrives in mayhem and uses it to his own advantage, amen!

To be prepared for war is one of the most effectual means of ensuring peace. George Washington

These people are like dumbed down wild animals. There is no reasoning with them and they are implacable.

Trump's not moving fast enough--hurry up, roll it all out!

The media is a nonstop barrage of negative news about our president.

Where the left sees "discrimination" the right sees "safety and protection".

Sitcoms throw entire programming into leftist indoctrination. Putting down fathers and moms up, fornication.

Liberals heads are spinning right now. Gaga didn't trash Trump but just did her job and entertained us all.

They said "he says outrageous things" but everything he said rang true to me--like a bell that rings.

The very tribe lost without you may ban you cuz they have that to learn: appreciation of all and why you do.

Dems would rather keep failed policies in place then put a qualified person in to do what we want, ok?

President wants to keep us safe but the fake news says "it's all ok--there are NO terrorist attacks, no way."

BOOMERS AND BROKENNESS

CHILDISH DEMOCRATS ARE LOSING LUSTER

Childish democrats are quickly losing luster: Delay, run the clock out, not come to hearings, filibuster.

The left favors feel good sentiment over safety, guilt assuagement over decency.

Trump'll smash political correctness, safe spaces and trigger warning culture and liberate us from the vulgar.

The right is all about safety, the left: "let em all in" and it will always be that way though obviously wrong ok?

Trump: even one killed is too much. Left: don't stereotype, don't judge!

How powerful standing up in a room full of leftists and spew libtard platitudes to applause while being rude.

Safety precautions are now "mean spirited" rather than just common sense in this generation (so dense).

See the past as "the war". It was your mal-adaptation to liberalism, a mental illness leaving you scarred and poor.

The social hypnotism of liberalism lays groundwork for abortions, divorces, addictions, heresies, debaucheries.

We have to forgive em (they were possessed by social hypnotism to believe a lie) but many were hurt, oh my.

Every hurt, every evil memory comes down to "liberalism is a sickness" and I must remember this, then diss.

All states are different and some are riddled through and through with liberalism. Move for exhilarating escapism.

Been through so much with the election and now this: people are quitting the news now--it's all dissed.

TWO AMERICAS: CRAZY COASTS & HAPPY FARMERS

BOOMERS AND BROKENNESS

There are two Americas: the crazy coasts and the happy holy farmers in the middle, the guideposts.

Social hypnotism can consume a state till everyone you meet's a liberal or justice warrior filled with hate.

My war was California liberalism while not realizing it, thinking it was me. Then moved to Utah/feel so free!

The left is organizing fight clubs to go out and kill "nazis" which is you, me, us.

University of California is trying to divert attention from the looming pedophilia raids (e.g. Penn State).

To grow up in a sheltered religious household then exposed to and controlled by liberalism was so cold.

At UCI I was hit on by professors in the most crude ways--won't stop talking about it to the end of my days.

CULTURAL PSYCHOLOGY IN STATES

There's a cultural psychology to every state. Re-adaptation is your therapy as you geographically relocate.

Both coasts = crazy. Go inner, be happy.

Burning with with self-flattery they seek to keep us down. That's the nature of tyranny: hating the renowned.

They're hoping you don't want the fight but if you persist you'll win cuz they're little demons (low soul-height).

Fox is sneaky how they put down Trump. The Murdock sons are running things and they're liberals (crud).

Every time they say our guy falls down in the mud he always comes up smelling like roses twice as much!

Though they call him obnoxious, bombastic and irritating we love him.

BOOMERS AND BROKENNESS

Even Michael Savage is putting our leader down--I'm turning em all off now.

Our guy has a heart. That's altogether different from the sadistic fake-nice of the apathetic (with smiles large).

GREAT LEADERS CAN TAKE IT

They speak against Trump and I get sad. Then he snaps back—so bad--and I'm happy again, so glad!

The democrats were the slave owners and the KKK. They're mean spirited but covered by a "nice" identity.

He knows what we went through--he feels sympathy. So refreshing after experiencing cold smiling apathy.

If you trust Fox and suddenly they throw you a zinger against your winner it hurts, it's disconcerting, a bummer.

Divorces happening as libtard wives disgusted with Trumpist husbands. Good riddance, be gone hons'

Dems are choking on loser's tears, embarrassment, questioning, deflation, humiliation and self-effacement.

Leftists' rhetoric appeases their anti-Trump agenda at all cost, regardless that our safety is lost.

They're bringing themselves down. Arrogance before the fall, last ditch efforts, implosion/panic: clowns.

They hate any anomaly like a conservative homosexual/black. No mental flex: don't fit the matrix, reject.

Overthrowing the bill of rights and the constitution is NOT free speech but outright illegal and sedition.

Piers Morgan knows he was defeated and is now crawling back acting like he's one of us the newly elited.

OLD HIPPIES NEVER GIVE UP

BOOMERS AND BROKENNESS

Americans rejected your failed leftist policies and now you wanna obstruct plans of our elected president?

To Pocahontas and leftist friends: if your judge-shopping and obstructing results in terrorism it's your end.

Mag shows Trump cutting of head of liberty by doing what 4 presidents have done but now it's a tragedy?

They never give up building a case against Trump (to not be seen as wrong) can you believe this stuff?

The amount of subversion against Trump is astounding, even leaking rats in the whitehouse are obstructing.

Trump studies everything all night long. He catches on, he always comes back/wins against the evil throng.

POLITICS TO KEEP INFERIOR OUT

Get into politics so inferior men can't rule over you. That means to look good, be good, study and pray too

"He shouldn't criticize judges" when there've been arrests of supreme court justices all through the ages.

Stop listening/repeating their spiel. It's all bull, easily disproven, unreal.

End of phoniness: Elizabeth Warren (Pocahontas) getting on her high horse with pure race-baiting of course.

FOX: cacophonous, interruptive, frustrating, boring, aggravating! Few pearls interjected keeps ya comin'

Fake news: Not just omissions but wrong priorities, focus or trivializations

Comeback Trump: As dems sue his every move we must wait for his win over those who disapprove.

We elected him for his sly smarts. Once aware he cleans house so hold on for great changes to start.

BOOMERS AND BROKENNESS

Donald since they're gonna slam you for everything just ignore it all, do your thing

They put our lives at risk just for politics.

Ignore the anti-Trumpers cuz they're just paid protestors.

GEORGE SOROS BIG BUX TO SAY TRUMP SUX

Soros pays big bux to make it look like Trump sux but it's all lies, he's deluxe.

Sickening stupidity of the arrogant confirmed by the money they make in their leftist liberal element.

It's a lie to omit, distort or de-prioritize focus but that's the leftist pundits in their verbal hocus-pocus.

They're making it look like the mentally ill protests are much bigger than they are. Plan: villainize our star.

People are so used to being pushed around mentally it's all about "agreement" and it's embarrassing.

Marriages are breaking up over Trump.

9th circus has 90% reversal rate. They're the ones who outlawed U.S. flag shirts--arrest them like did Abe.

National sovereignty and the flag is now racism. That's how far we've gone into mental illness and barbarism.

Iranians shouting "death to America" aligned with the left against Trump: think about that--aren't they crud?

Trump is not like Hitler. Just because a leader wants order doesn't mean they're like a dictator. Marion Andrews

Why aren't feminists fighting for mutilated Pakistani women? We're so lucky to have gentle American men.

BOOMERS AND BROKENNESS

Micro aggressions aren't coming to your gender but lack of refinement and class: be a lady not an ass.

Tradition has it he'll always be called "president" but for all his many, many crimes he should be arrested.

California wants money. Trump: shut down sanctuary cities, deport illegals and fight campus violence honey.

Libs outraged that Ivanka wore the dress she made, but not that the Clinton Foundation paid and played?

A society that cannot defend its children has no future. Vladimir Putin

The Christian life is a wonderful exciting journey. Dr. Charles Stanley

SWEPT UP INTO PC CULTURE: DON'T KNOW ANY BETTER

They didn't know any better. They were swept up into fear-laden PC culture so forgive even the vultures.

What the man has promised he's done so shut up libs he's only begun.

Transgender suicide rate is 40%. Go against biology = torment.

People who kill people should be killed but babies who are innocent should not.

Faulty thinking: taking the marginal case and applying it to all. Abortion's not about rape/incest, that's small.

Today's democrats are immature, entitled and crazy--yet to grow up.

We've fought too long to be pulled back by small jealous women too limited to comprehend our advances. Judge Jeanine

Because of our blind cultural relativism we had to have millions here for a season but now they'll be leavin'.

25% of all college students have been diagnosed with a mental disorder. A giant brainwashing facility, horror.

BOOMERS AND BROKENNESS

Save your money and don't send kids to college. Fake degrees, no jobs and messed up with no knowledge.

VICTIMIZED IDENTITY CAN'T SUCCEED

Being diagnosed gives them a license to not study, work, succeed and that's their victimhood identity.

Diagnoses are awards that change status or expectations towards.

A pharmaceutical force has taken over the young and given rise to insane behavior courtesy of big pharma.

Being over-diagnosed prevents them from going through rites of passages and growth. Crisis, synthesis, rise above.

Colleges are pharmaceutically controlled: psychiatric clinics and captives of the pharma cartel--it's cold.

The fact that so many hate Trump explains why I've felt so outa sync

Overwhelming but with Trump things change--the sea parts--and there's a comeback as he punts over them.

They'll even drop friends who don't share their hatred of Trump.

Become a Trump-hater just to join the club or not be snubbed--what a dud.

They felt superior for so long being a part of this liberal thing there is no way they could be proven wrong.

The more people believe it the less it's true.

Fake supermen: not fighting bad guys but fighting for good nonetheless.

Prosperity makes monsters, adversity makes men. Alex Jones

Soros bankrolled anti-Trump protests--just point out the fraud then reject.

Losers stay arrogant but shaky--can't accept it, get more flaky.

BOOMERS AND BROKENNESS

They want to extinguish thinkers--a bright light in a room full of vampires.

Elites are throwing everything they've got against Trump.

Being so immature they can't get straight but continue to push, harass, violently protest, aggravate, bait.

IT'S SOLITUDE VS. SOCIAL

It's solitude vs. social.

Obama was nice on surface but devil underneath (this they can't see) while Donald is just himself, free.

To face how wrong they are on Trump would mean to face how wrong an entire generation was--they can't!

Patriots need to street-preach liberty, bill of rights and constitution now.

Anti-Trump fervor: hysterical derangement.

Emptiness seeks company, fullness is distracted and bored by it: wants solitude for richness/profundity.

Crazy in, crazy out. If the dominant culture is liberal we adapt through mental illness without a doubt.

Insanity is a mal-adaptation to liberalism.

"It's all good" means "there is no justice" and that unnerves the righteous to the core so many seek solace.

To face what Hillary is is to face who they have been as hippies.

Clouded by dogma they can't see--like Merkel ruining her country.

Fascistic dogma systems are more like clubs, the mentality of mobs

Virtue signaling (act out goodness) comes off stilted like fake news.

BOOMERS AND BROKENNESS

We cannot allow a minority of people to hold a viewpoint that terrorizes the majority. Hillary Clinton

Since liberalism was the default setting in society and schools, conservatives were the minority, very un-cool.

MAINSTREAM MEDIA IS THE ENEMY

The mainstream media is the enemy, Trump's poll #s are surging cuz we all know the media is deceiving.

He'll make rich those who bitch then we'll unify in the American niche.

I know the truth so why study all the detractors? Return to the moment for it's YOUR great life that matters.

The party line is not legit: To fit hate Trump, hate Trump and you fit.

I like Milo (he's an intellectual) but why must he say such dirty things? Bad example by a Christian.

Don't study Trump detractors anymore. Life's too short/a waste of precious time: He won and they're a bore.

Liberals are so ideologically committed, rabid and terrified of the future they can't accept our new leader.

You don't wanna talk to me cuz I'm so much smarter and I prove all your false narratives wrong. Owen Shroyer

I have a right to offend you under the first amendment.

They're fast to police conservatives and slow to police progressives.

Sin is a mal-adaptive coping device in dense environments.

Price-payoff systems: People repent of the sin when the price becomes too high for the payoff--hitting bottom.

Liberalism: all-bull easily disproven but it can mess up your life for decades as society's default setting.

BOOMERS AND BROKENNESS

Liberalism is a religion with mantras. All bull, easily disproven but they'll kill you if you question it or mutter.

Feminists complain about "mansplaining" (yet they have it so good) while ignoring Islamic women and raping.

Fake news: I don't give em a chance to disappoint me like that--it's always like a stab in the back.

Trump: In 30 days more small business success than in 25 years.

LOSERS CAN'T GET OVER IT

Left is losing so will be increasingly violent. That's the dregs: vehement.

Whenever the left is vulnerable/going to get caught, they blame you for what they did. Loving: not.

The ineffectual are now aced out.

Left is face of disdainful superiority and virtue-signaling, but as they're aced out there's a quickening!

Fake news is trying to ruin our future, make us poor and divide the country more.

The spirit of 1776: Christ is the fulcrum, God is the father and the Holy Spirit is the delivery system. Alex Jones

Ideologues are always afraid of truth and thus they must banish it

Once free speech is gone your world turns dark with no escape.

Right to criticize and offend is the bulwark of western democracy.

Propaganda media vs. America

The media did not create Donald Trump and they can't destroy him. Rush Limbaugh

BOOMERS AND BROKENNESS

Liberalism has been the default setting since the sixties and these are the grandchildren of the hippies.

He didn't "delegitimize" the press--they did it to themselves.

Media's losing ratings as everything they say is Trump-hating.

We hate the media cuz it's so biased and corrupt.

TRUMP-HATE PUTS EM OUT OF GRACE

If everything they say/do/create is based on Trump-hate they'll be out of grace (disgraced) while we ace.

If you just talk issues, he's fine. But if you attack he becomes a pit bull--what a wonderful president of mine!

Trumpism reneged on every value someone under 35 had: Total trauma was the result and they're still mad.

Milo you're not a conservative since we are down-home family people guarding ears of children, you villain.

I had Stockholm Syndrome--caved when they pulled me down, gutted my identity: I was empty and unrenowned.

They always show their immaturities on TV so don't worry we'll win eventually.

Milo made remarks in his lectures to tempt boys to sleep with him. Not a conservative, friends!

Warning: The losers are so immature they can't accept it/may get violent.

The enemedia is dead: long live the people.

Stop your shameless virtue signaling about how progressive you are.

The media can turn on or off an entire culture. If fake we become rank, If saints we prosper/break the bank.

IT'S A SPIRITUAL FIGHT: GOOD VS. EVIL

BOOMERS AND BROKENNESS

Instead of living in utopian vision you gotta be prepared for what could happen.

Let the First lady be the new model of the superior woman supplanting the feminist avatar which is ugly.

In media (gov) complex people with logic are driven out--only party-liners remain.

Americans don't care about whiny, privileged multi-millionaire players' (brats) tiresome virtue signaling.

I was hammered mercilessly, made fun of, marginalized. John Moore

Like health, happiness is an earned state.

The spoiled child given no boundaries becomes a demanding monster like the kids at Berkeley or others.

An earned state goes against our immediate pleasures in time until tastes and appetites are refined.

Reason for rules is to avoid negative consequences: remove the consequences, no more rules.

BOOMERS: CONSEQUENCELESS HEDONISM

Despair of consequenceless hedonism: Irresponsibility is "self-expression" and self-restraint "repression".

You can't rebuild when all rules of self-restraint look like irrational neurotic repression, a mistake.

That's the world we live in, we're to accept this: everyone's a disease or victim in a Tower of Babble.

Follow the straight and narrow makes sense if you're walking on the beam not if just walking along, see?

BOOMERS AND BROKENNESS

Our enemies are college professors and journalists. They are creating this absurd reality, what a mess.

We're being censured but take it as a complement. If afraid of our words it means we're dominant.

We're not haters, we have restraint. "Sexists, racists"--recall the 80's when mesmerized by Soul Train.

The blacks on Soul Train dressed beautifully and danced with ingenuity but now that's racist--really?

No sexism in the West but plenty in the East and Islam but with liberals that's never addressed.

LIBERALS PAINT A FALSE REALITY

They're painted a false reality like the whole country's in slavery and none of it's true believe me.

The immature minds, I don't blame them much. It's the strings behind the blind that are out to lunch.

We are quickly becoming post-Christian society and soon will be minority but still it's True Reality.

They just can't express anger without swearing and instantly their power is gone and it's boring.

They took young minds, which are idealistic/easily energized, and created communism disguised.

JP Rowling author of Harry Potter occult trend is pushing anti-depressants and grooming depression.

Whatever doesn't kill you makes you stronger. They're turning you into absolute basketcase victims sir.

Churchhill was depressed but so focused with his job of saving the west he never caved into this test.

BOOMERS AND BROKENNESS

They are the whiney millennial entitled society deserving of fame and fortune just for being born.

Anti-depressant usage up 400% over 20 years. It makes em wanna-be yes-people, zombies, careless.

50 years ago depression was "temporary unhappiness" not this lifelong illness for big pharma bucks.

Labeling Theory: You've bought the big lie and even let em poison you, making you a blank zombie.

WHINERS ARE MALADAPTIVE LOSERS

In the frontier depression got you killed or starved. You had to work to stay alive, no time for that jive.

Depression label is the externalization that allows them to avoid responsibility for their life.

Depression: In all cases there's nothing wrong with brain just outlook in life and therapist directs strife.

One generation prospers and the next are debauched, neurotic, self-involved, hypnotized failures.

Psychiatry and profit motive: Keep em coming back. Many women fall for their therapist, that's a fact.

Depression comes from not being in the groove. Find out what you do best and it's all removed.

You are not a victim but they are telling you to surrender, take these pills and succumb.

Criminalization of political differences endangers democracy. Alan Dershowitz

Liberals are not logical so just forget em, don't entangle--this is critical.

It's not that Milo's rude, but crude. Talking about sex too much sullies his message and intrudesTop of Form

BOOMERS AND BROKENNESS

Stop talking about sex Milo. You're destroying your worthy message and godly will see you as foe.

Milo says he's a victim not a defender of perversion, ok fine but why talk so dirty in conversations?

Kids may be sexualized but us elder Christians are not so kindly clean your speech of this perverse rot!

EVEN GRANDMOTHERS TALK ROT

If you wanna know how to act/talk, emulate great grandmother cuz even grandmother may be rot.

It's been three generations of this crap so clean the slate to essentially: just your own map.

Churches must be totally protected to say "No, we're not marrying two men/two women, no way".

There's male and female, birds and the bees. There's no way you can re-organize this and stay free.

They act like this is all settled--it's not. We'll fight until the old paths are restored and we're rid of rot.

If they wanna settle down/build a life together, fine--a civil arrangement not churches forced in line.

Society is reorganized for the worst by crazy human rights courts.

Where are the "white supremacists"? We just wanna live our own lives but liberals create a nuisance.

This is you being devilish and crude not "unsayable truths".

Even though wrong, a movement explodes through youth throngs and just for kicks more come along.

First amendment means you have the right to argue about things without being called names.

BOOMERS AND BROKENNESS

Antifa says the most victimized are the most legitimized, but the truth is: whites are most despised.

The more victimized the more legitimized so white males are at the bottom as the hated "privileged".

OPINIONS ARE SIMPLY GROUP IDENTITY

Value of opinion is based on group identity so if I don't like your ideas I'm attacking you personally?

Words are "micro-aggressions" attacking you personally. So you've a right to get violent at me?

You don't have to prove you're micro-aggressed, all that is required is your *feeling* of offense.

The rich are not making you poor, they're paying your salary. Ben Shapiro

A generation of women have been told a baby's a polyp so they don't hate abortion or work to stop it.

A whole generation actually thinks it's not killing a child but removing a tumor: it's good, it's clever.

More they preach love, goodness, fairness the more violent we become: it's virtue signaling vs. the One.

You can't prosecute them due to intent: They really think it's a polyp not a baby/they're made dense.

Forces in society vs. the individual trying to forge a way above the trends creating prevalent insanity.

Democracy is the worst system except for all the others. Winston Churchill

Avoid lasciviousness. To know how to act think of great-grandparents cuz 3 generations are bad.

Kids may be sexualized but us elder Christians are not, so kindly clean your speech of this perverse rot!

BOOMERS AND BROKENNESS

College administrators are the problem, caving into this and also radical faculty which are absurdly leftist.

HOW TO ADAPT TO CRAZIES: ISOLATION

The only way to adapt to the crazies was to go into total isolation or become part of them.

Guilt religion coming from Marxism (racism, race-baiting) is bringing down the west which is the best.

Denounce liberal terrorism before it's too late.

PC culture is an ideology rooted in constant new oppressions and finding new enemies to maintain power/aggressions

Kids are crazy with all their genders. They don't know a thing about politics but are communist defenders.

How dare your daughter not wanna see a man's genitals. They're priming for pedophilia and it's getting old.

"Your kids belong to us and we're getting rid of the family". The family breaks down in this engineered reality.

If you go along with this crap (e.g. gender) you'll lose the map of essentials for happiness: old ways are best.

Cops blocked by liberal mayors/can't deport killers: Libs don't care about you and that's why we're bitter.

Their weapons are of no avail. Over goodness and God's will evil will not prevail.

The deluge of Trump-hate demonstrates the degree of mental illness in states. Russophobic insanity has taken over.

The left was looking forward to a Hillary Clinton presidency to finish America off for good: that was trendy.

BOOMERS AND BROKENNESS

Kids that didn't get what they wanted for birthday so get violent about it: that's the left (and they don't quit).

Alinsky: Accuse others of what you are doing. Dems have been in bed with Russia for 50 years and Hillary's selling.

The backbone/decent people of America must stand up against the bitter people of the entertainment industry.

EASILY BEND A DEMORALIZED POPULATION

Demoralize the population cuz when they don't have morals you can bend them as you please.

Left: Left-hand path, Luciferianism, Satanism, devil worshippers.

The Satanists are in huge rallies against Trump who has invoked God.

Fake media: deceptive, hateful enemy of the people. Globalist, evil.

The media is connected to the ruling class, the deep state, Soros and that's why you can't believe em, sorry.

They get off on you not having something.

Beck's paid/protected like Hillary and Obama. They don't get into trouble but Trump may end their bubble.

You're bad cuz you freaked out at a man in the bathroom. They sexualize kids by removing gender (doom).

I don't care Milo what you say, you said pederasty was all-ok.

Our man's at the Whitehouse working not at frivolous events smirking.

We'll do as we wilt. Witches Law on Trump-haters
Milo the reprobate debauched fallen soul: sudden fall, that's all.

Fire Bill Maher and ban him from TV. He said a boy age 14 raped by female teacher age 35 was all-ok.

BOOMERS AND BROKENNESS

They call him "Hitler" though Hitler killed millions and Trump just regulations.

Men respond to the attraction factors of women but are repelled if distasteful/non-nurturing (mother).

Lame media: Stop reporting on how you feel bad cuz no one cares.

NEW MCCARTHYISM

We are in a new McCarthyism more frightening than ever before. Lionel

Demonize them, marginalize them, polarize them, spread hatred and tell lies about the opposition: Alinsky/Lenin.

Liberals, universities, media, professional protestors and Hollywood are all against him: stand against them.

Synagogues of Satan: faith communities, interfaith dialogue, Chrislam, Unity--Christianity is exclusivity.

Obama was about "cut outs" from laws (exemptions for buddies) but Trump is the rule of law in reality.

Everything Trump has done is existing law.

The first attack against Donald Trump was fired only a few minutes into the Oscars then they kept on coming.

Stick a fork in the dinosaur mainstream media: they're done. Alex Jones

Washington Post, Newsweek, Time call for insurrection/murder of the president--of course he's blocking em.

Anti-God, anti-family: at the bottom of the left is occultism/sex abuse and it easily turns violent too.

We're done with the Oscars, Hollywood and public schools. We're the new inventors and now we're cool.

New religion is political correctness, globalism and break up families and nations--bunch of blobs with no elation.

BOOMERS AND BROKENNESS

The best thing about Trump is he's not out to get us. Alex Jones

God hates cowards, abusers of innocence or those weaker than them. That's scripture so be a leader, friend.

The most disenfranchised people under globalism are the ones saying "kill Trump": it's really amazing stuff.

Get em stultified on social issues that are never rectified while meanwhile they're gang-raped with lies.

The most hated are Glenn Beck and Megyn Kelly. There's just something about a turncoat that's smelly.

SYCOPHANTS READING OFF SCRIPT

Whoopie and sycophants reading off a script then selling their tyranny and lies: that's Hollywood scum you guys.

Actors pushing leftist crap and they don't even believe it. Doing what they're told or insane mentals getting old.

The Oscar anti-Trump fiasco with each star seeing who could get in the biggest jab at our commander-in-chief.

They're not just declaring war on Trump but everyone who voted for him.

Arrogance: "Our goal in politics is the same as our goal in art, and that's to get to the truth." Warren Beatty

How could demented Hollywood applaud Iran who kills gays/beheads jews?

Hollywood never thinks of the victims of Iran--they just love it, man.

Leftists are not morons they're evil anti-American, anti-individual liberty, pro-collective controlling globalists.

If liberals were morons they couldn't make a dent like this, proving the wrong premise overrides intelligence.

BOOMERS AND BROKENNESS

Projecting adulthood on babies is criminal, and treating adults as babies is terrible, the worst of all.

He talks like someone who doesn't understand it (BS) but wants to sound like someone who does.

LIBERAL HOGWASH: JOY, LOVE & HAPPINESS

Always talking about joy and happiness sounds like a liberal because that's the spiel but it's unreal.

Facing the ugly truth is our only defense. Living in la la land leaves you unprotected: need gate/fence.

Afro-centered or women's studies just teach lies with no accountability so they hate white society.

Arrogant professors, like we're supposed to take on their jargon when it's all so contrived/far out.

Loving liberal females are now often slipping into pugnacity: duking it out with other loving ladies.

They think there's only one prism to see the world: social justice--all is homophobic, racist or sexist.

In everything they do they're searching for a bigot. Two warring parties: which one (can you dig it)?

"Where's the bigot" is so fatuous, stupid, reductionist and depressing. Milo

Socialist deep need for equality, lack of competition and unconditional love transferred to state (GOV).

"Safe" spaces break down barriers between words and action--like there's something trying to hurt them.

Lower IQs cling to repetition to gain security--they don't know what's going on, it's virtual reality.

BOOMERS AND BROKENNESS

Poorly educated shallow thinkers cling to slogans and superficial sayings and thoughts: stinkers.

Family breakup due to feminism, media male-bashing and courts. It's eugenics/globalism of course.

ONLY THE DUMB ARE RABBLE-ROUSED

The dumb, uneducated or brainwashed are easily rabble-roused, feeling smart even when soused.

The male bashing is relentless while TV movies show their supposed violence against innocence.

Men are bigger and trained for war so of course it's easy to make them seem like evil monsters.

Everyone takes her side because that's these times and it's all confirmed (continuously) with TV lies.

Men I've known just wanna get along. Peace at any price in fact, they just want tranquility with woman.

One neurotic female pattern is recurrent eruptions out of nowhere. Ladies stay sweet and have flair.

Men want tranquility, women want security--but government supports them so why stay skinny?

Looking healthy and fit for her man: that's called fat-shaming now and it's ok to look like a van.

After gender studies they're dumber than when they started--less capable of real world/hardhearted.

Everyone's mad these days: angry, drunk or insane. It's far better to be alone to avoid this drain.

She lost her job due to sexism, not cuz she was late or made messes.

BOOMERS AND BROKENNESS

Modern education has replaced intellectual humility with dogma and it's boring, we don't want ya.

Social justice cult graduates and think they have nothing left to learn--all comes down to being burned.

SPOT THE BIGOT!

"Spot the Bigot": That is the focus of every page, sitcom and newscast and we have had it.

Never having a kid's job they aren't happy in the free market and say "I'm oppressed", oh yah.

Western liberal capitalist democracies are where you need to be if you are gay, female, black: free.

The left is more superstition than religion because facts don't matter to them so they never give in.

Love, sacrifice and giving are the highest virtues to Christians but are a laugh to the undisciplined.

They don't care about women they're just being used as tool for central planning and collectivism.

Marketing ploy: Don't you care about women's rights/equality? But it's all collectivism and globalist lies.

They get along fine then she sees a feminist friend and turns on husband, going way over the line.

For fifty years women have become more miserable as they become more "equal". Why, ingratitude?

A good man is self-sacrificing and generous but now they say feminists have "used all that against us".

In this rabid anti-male environment ridiculous rape claims are heeded no matter how virulent.

BOOMERS AND BROKENNESS

Studies show women are 10 X more likely to forgive a terrorist, see him as good or blame his childhood.

Students infected with micro-aggression mentality: attack my politics and it's violence against my identity.

SPEECH IS VIOLENT? WE WON'T BE SILENT

"Speech is violent, we will not be silent" more BS by the millennial moronic.

I'll never forget the abuses visited upon us by the progressive left.

The Krazy Kollege Kids are ultra-conformists not free thinkers tho' they fancy themselves in those terms.

Thinking man is good they think nothing of coming to your door and inviting all their friends over.

The founders of this country were Calvinists, Puritans and then cowboys and none trusted humans!

Trump is called bigoted, hateful, malevolent. It's just the opposite, he loves America/not out to get us.

It's true they're brainwashed but still their lower self came out and yuk what a gross draught.

The left envies the raw power Islamic governments have over their people-- connection is gov not religion--evil.

Liberals admire how they ruthlessly rule--hating the constitution and human rights they learned in school.

These people are dead, we can't work with them. Trump won, he's our only hope so go inside/ignore dopes.

Dopes don't realize how many of us there are. They'll find out soon, we've got real political power.

LEFT ALIGNS WITH IRAN

BOOMERS AND BROKENNESS

How is it the left can't see how vacuous they are dangerously aligning the terror state with the "stars".

Applauding Iran who executes gays and chops off hands. Drug-addicted perverts: the Hollywood scam.

The leftists are complete fascists and will always reject. They're on the dark side but not the elect.

Why don't celebs vacation in Iran? They're like snotty lowlife sophomoric college kids and pro-Islam

They don't have the intellectual ability to see what they've done funded by Iran.

You put down America for cruelty but Iran hangs gays from cranes.

Hollywood is heavily homosexual yet loves Iran who kills gays, well?

Hollywood: poor acting, scumbag morals, sell out fakes--silly mistakes.

Zombies can't think they can only recite by rote

Divide and conquer: Call him "Hispanic" because that's what he is, not "Latino" cuz that is political.

Just love God, no more tears: I learned this in a tiny cabin on one thousand acres in the desert wilderness for 27 years.

FRUIT AND GRAINS

Never thought I'd say it but I've ended up on corn, beans, rice with salsa on it. Other than that fruit and juices.

Not interested in greens, just get the job done--fill the tank to get back to work. That's what it's all about first.

Fruit, rice, beans, corn and salsa--like every other human culture on this continent with satiety power.

BOOMERS AND BROKENNESS

You wouldn't see a cowboy fooling around with greens or fruit. It's satiety power/calorie density not sparsity.

I'm thru killing myself, of writhing in bed all day in pain. Fruit, fruit, salad and sometimes high-fat avo days.

I'm thru living on alka-seltzer/ant-acids. They're only temporary, eventually you must face the foods.

Everyone has ups and downs but when you're dwelling on stuff--psycho-aggressive consistently--it's diet.

There's no lukewarm see. I want warm cashmere or cotton/rayon cami but nothing in between.

ARNOLD EHRET: ACID IS MUCUS

Water, apple juice, melon, mango smoothie, rice with salsa. Enjoy the magnificent views without acid.

Toxic ACID crystals the basis of wrinkles, what is the biggest reason for acid? FATS, no longer on our menu.

Old style prisons provided one menu: grease and pig fat in sawdust. To anything human beings can adapt.

Always have fruit first for breakfast and lunch then when you get to the starch it's appreciated and it satiates.

Ok, it's fruit or fast FIRST, consistently. Having rice or cereal for breakfast made me hungry all day and sleepy.

Let the starch be your REWARD or as a cheap thrill it won't even taste good. ACHIEVE your satisfaction.

If I start out in a fast or just juice I go into no-hunger work mode but if I eat starch first I feel useless/old.

Started to yearn for avo-satiety on the third day of the 811 diet, ready to give up--then suddenly LIT UP.

BOOMERS AND BROKENNESS

When she took so many supplements her face was bloated and broad, when not it went narrow and long.

Start with a smoothie, move into a salad and finish with grains if you must [they cause acid so it's better NOT].

PUMPERNICKLE IS ACID BINDING!

The only non-acid bread is pumpernickle. It goes good with salads and buttresses up your meals a little.

Yes refried vegetarian beans have zero fat but cause massive mucus/acid: that's why you feel like that.

If a food causes acid it causes MUCUS and that's the sticky stuff mucking up the works in ALL disease cases.

Medicine throughout history has seen disease as a matter of ACID. Everything but plants causes it.

Know all diets/reverse between to suit needs. Mucus-less [fruits/veg], fat/fruit [avo], low fat [inc. grains].

On my lowfat day I ate beans and thought I would die. Grains and beans are massive acid formers: bye bye.

Mucus from acid is not just nose/throat but all throughout and every cell is coated! It means wrinkles, bloat.

A totally acid/mucus-binding day: fruit smoothie with banana/berries, cantaloupe, salad: all ok.

Go non-acid [mucus-binding] and watch all wrinkles leave the body. God didn't mean that for us, surely.

It's not hard by taking one step at a time. Don't start with rice, you'll be hungry and tired--begin with a fruit high.

CORN AND SPUD ARE ACID BINDING

BOOMERS AND BROKENNESS

If you must eat starch after everything else, constrain to corn and spuds. Low acid/mucus: right on the cusp.

On my lowfat high-sugar day I thought I'd die from the beans, rice and cereal with the sugar piled high: yuk!

Durianrider can eat like that as an athlete who works it off but I lay in bed praying for death, it's like an assault.

Stay a petite little lady: fruit, fruit, salad and a LITTLE corn or spud if you must, just to round the meal off.

A little white rice with salsa, I'll constrain to that. Delicate digestion: with fibrous grains, don't take a chance.

When you eat something wrong it's like putting your ENEMY inside--to do his dastardly deeds as you die.

You eat something wrong and it's an EXPLOSION. The immune system says WTF, it's like a bomb.

They tell you to eat fruit then the massive mucus-producers like grains or beans. AVO tho' fat is better to me.

Reversal Diet between fruit/fat and fruit/starch. Cereal is with rice milk and raisons/cane sugar [acid-binding].

If you gotta have refried beans fill em with diced onions and lotsa salsa, then you're at least compensating.

When I resumed lowfat fruit diet I was so famished. Gotta add starch but fat is more satiety-effective.

Without fat you gotta eat 100 bananas to feel full and even then you don't feel satisfied--I think it's bull.

80-10-10 WORKS BEST? FRUIT/STARCH

Of all diets, fruit/GRAINS worked best. That's just me and I've tried em all--and this diet is raw and fresh.

BOOMERS AND BROKENNESS

Cereal with raisins and cane sugar doesn't last that long, for satiety I need avocado/olive oil activating glucagon.

They won't eat avo but will eat all those cooked refined acid-producing starches cuz it's "still 80-10-10".

Ok with lowfat now: love being a skinny gal. Cereal with rice milk, cane, raisins, collagen/frijoles with onions.

Fruit yah but I just wanna get filled up so I can get back to work. Calorie density, get the job done--see?

May have some fruit-FAT days later on but for now, I'm <10% fat and loving that=high sugar gets in the cells.

I feel high and alert, lovin' the earth: that's glucose in the cells cuz there's no fat to block that: like a pill.

Yah this is good, sugar in the cells unblocked by fat and no need for stimulants like coffee/things like that.

I'm a hard worker all day and night with only catnaps. I can't do all that on a fruit diet, I need starch or fat.

FRUIT AND CHEESE OR GRAINS

I can't have grapefruits then work all day long without intrusive hunger pains. Fruit diet: no way.

Lotsa fruit yes, but round it off with starch or fat. I wouldn't have em together you'll gain weight--alternate.

Last century people worked all day in the fields after having YAMS for breakfast--that makes more sense.

It's not that I don't like the fruit but that I don't have a place for it anymore. Apple juice if thirsty, grains/beans.

I thought fruit and fat diet worked best cuz FAT brings on the Dunning Kruger Effect of lower intellect.

BOOMERS AND BROKENNESS

AVO mucked up the works, I'm sure of it. I'll give it a year without it or any oils as I've adapted to lowfat.

JUST PERUSE YOUR WORK

Today just peruse YOUR work and attractions and you'll gain far more than boring grooves laid by factions.

My success is silently in my room devoted and immersed in my work, not out there wearing a smirk.

To succeed you must WORK at relationships. The work is biting your tongue and leaving out snide remarks.

If sex is the prize, the weapon is post-orgasmic withdrawal and a discard not just her refusing you guys.

LEAVE/cut him loose to live life more abundantly. Get into yourself and your own talents not that guy.

After spending a lifetime on your career it's unlikely you'll find a clone--just seek a pleasant, gentle, nice man.

Was it manipulation or precognition? Should she feel guilty or is it just she can see ahead as in synchronicity?

I prefer looking at it that way--I can see ahead, so it's not a threat. Man plans, God laughs--by Him I'm led.

I never want an identity of an old lady. I'm a creative spirit until my last day on earth and it's ageless baby.

BUT when you start talkin' like you do, ageist remarks etc--I get nervous and the archetypes change on this.

Decades of silence, dung, nothing happening. Then there is flowering, that means remuneration--harvesting.

For relief, concentrate on SELF only for awhile. No more political videos or searching exes on the sly.

BOOMERS AND BROKENNESS

YOUR work, your music videos, your movies, your home and views, what interests you, your body new.

KEEP WRITING UNTIL THAT MOMENT

All I can do is keep writing. The life God gave to me after overcoming things you wouldn't believe, a series.

I do nothing to promote it. God said He'd give me the LINK to success and I continue to write and wait for it.

You are my link/I am your link and it's a great and marvelous wonder how God works don't you think?

I'll write until that moment the universe opens up to the NEW LIFE of renowned success: I know it will be this.

My work must stand on its own. Not pumped thru interviews, explanations of it's meaning but just staying alone.

I'm sure not gonna ruin it by one false move or stupid word triggering a rash of liberal backlash on this nerd.

I'll put a wall around the whole property and create my own reality, loving every paradisiacal day until eternity.

We're all violators because we've all been violated and that is society. Dr. Steve Turley.

The line between good and evil cuts through every human heart. Aleksandr Solzhenitsyn.

THE HERD IN WORDS
HIX POLITIX
HOW THEY RUINED US
JUST SKIP DINNER
LE FEMME AND THE COMMUNIST SPIRIT
LIBERAL CHAOS & ROT
LIBERAL DOUBLETHINK
LIBERAL GALL 1 & 2
LIBERAL SHOVE-DOWNS
LOCK YOUR GATE
LOSERS and Femme Fatales
MANUAL FOR SUPERIOR MEN
MODERN ART FROM HELL
MOSTLY FAKE
NOTES TO CHAMPS 1 & 2
OVERCOME FRENEMIES
PC MAKES US CRAZY
PEOPLE ARE CRUEL
PEOPLE PROBLEMS 1 & 2
PERSECUTED GENIUIS
POLI-PSYCH MYSTERIES
PRETENTIOUS SLOBS
QUEEN BEE
RED NEW DEAL
RETURNING TO FIRST NATURE
SEASON OF TREASON
SEPARATE MEANS HOLY
SOCIAL HYPNOTISM
SOLITUDE SOLUTION
SUPERCILIOUS
THE SCHOOLS SCREWED EM UP
TOAD TO PRINCE
TRIALS CYCLES
TRUMP VS. GROUP
TRUST IN TRASH
THE TRUTH ABOUT PEOPLE
UNDERHEANDEDLY CLEVER
WALK TALL WITHIN WALLS
WE'RE NOT ALL ONE
WINNERS SKIP DINNER
WORK OR SMERK

100 KAREN KELLOCK BOOKS

AFFINITY OR MISERY
AGELESS CORNUCOPIA
AMERICA AWAKE!
AMERICA'S DAFT ERA
ARTS OF PALEO FASTING
AUTOPHAGY ON CHEATERS
BACKSTABBING NEUROTICS
BETRAYAL TRAUMA
BOOMERS AND BROKENNESS
BOOT ON NECK
CHAMPION GUIDES
COMMIE NUTHOUSE
COMMIES
COMMUNIST SPIRIT
CONTAGION OF MADNESS
CONTAGIOUS MADNESS
CULTURE CLASH BASHED
DAFT LEFT
DAILY FASTARIAN
DAM RATS
DIVERSITY IS CRUELTY
E-RACE WHITE
EVIL FREAKS (Beyond Gross)
THE END OR A BEND?
FEMALE BULLIES AND FEMI-NAZIS
FEMALE CARNALITY
FEMALE DUMB DOWN
FEMALE POWER DRIVE
FEMINISM AND RUIN 1 & 2
FIX FOR MISFITS
FOOLS & TRAMPS
FREEDOM SPEAKING
FRENEMY ENABLER
FRENEMY LIAR
FRENEMY THIEF
FRENEMY TRAITOR
TRENEMY TYRANT
GENIUS IS HELD DOWN
GLOBALISLAM
GOD USES THE FLAWED
HAZE OF THE LATTER DAYS

KAREN KELLOCK PH.D.

M.S. Political Science, San Diego State. Ph.D. in Psychology, University of California Irvine. Postdoctoral: UCI School of Medicine, Dept. of Psychiatry [NIMH Grants]. Developed the Debris Theory of Disease, a theory of system pathology in 120 books and 22 textbooks for the general public. The theory has a general formula: All disease is obstruction, all recovery is elimination, all success is attraction. The three obstructions are people, habit and food. Remove obstruction and snap to your goals, waiting in the wings.